How to

manage

your boss

Books to make you better

Books to make you better. To make you *be* better, *do* better, *feel* better. Whether you want to upgrade your personal skills or change your job, whether you want to improve your managerial style, become a more powerful communicator, or be stimulated and inspired as you work.

Prentice Hall Business is leading the field with a new breed of skills, careers and development books. Books that are a cut above the mainstream – in topic, content and delivery – with an edge and verve that will make you better, with less effort.

Books that are as sharp and smart as you are.

Prentice Hall Business.
We work harder – so you don't have to.

For more details on products, and to contact us, visit
www.business-minds.com
www.yourmomentum.com

ROS JAY

How to manage your boss

Developing the perfect working relationship

Prentice
Hall

BUSINESS

an imprint of Pearson Education

London • New York • Toronto • Sydney • Tokyo • Singapore • Hong Kong • Cape Town

New Delhi • Madrid • Paris • Amsterdam • Munich • Milan • Stockholm

PEARSON EDUCATION LIMITED

Edinburgh Gate
Harlow CM20 2JE
Tel: +44 (0)1279 623623
Fax: +44 (0)1279 431059

Website: www.pearsoned.co.uk

First published in Great Britain in 2002

ISBN: 978-0-273-65931-0

British Library Cataloguing in Publication Data
A CIP catalogue record for this book can be obtained from the British Library

10 9 8 7

Designed by Claire Brodmann Book Designs, Lichfield, Staffs.
Typeset by Northern Phototypesetting Co. Ltd, Bolton
Printed and bound in Great Britain

The Publishers' policy is to use paper manufactured from sustainable forests.

Contents

Part III ② How to manage a difficult boss

Introduction

Your relationship with your boss is probably the most important relationship you have at work. So it needs to be excellent. You don't have to be best mates outside working hours, but you do need to get on well at work, and to trust and respect each other personally and professionally. The better you understand each other, the more enjoyable, easy and rewarding it will be working together.

A good boss will be working hard at this relationship, and you need to work at it too. Not only will the relationship be far better if you are both giving it your best, but you are in a position to make the biggest contribution. After all, you have only one direct boss (or perhaps two at most) to concentrate on, while your boss may have several team members to build relationships with. If you're also a manager yourself, you'll recognise this difference in your approach between your boss and your team members.

And in the end, you have more to lose if the relationship doesn't gel. You rely on your boss for motivation, support, pay rises, promotion, even the fact that you have a job in the organisation at all. Your boss doesn't need you as badly as you need them. It stands to reason, then, that the onus is on you to make sure that you and your boss make a great team.

A good boss will be working hard at this relationship, and you need to work at it too.

The first thing you need to do is to get inside your boss's head. If you don't understand what makes them tick, you can't hope to understand how to manage them.

Managing your boss is all about making their relationship with you simple and rewarding. The aim is that the boss should look up with pleasure when you walk into the room, knowing that you'll be easy to get on with, co-operative, positive, reliable and trustworthy. If you and your boss both fit this description already, you're very lucky. What is more likely is that you'll get on in certain areas but there will be others where your work styles clash or your personalities sometimes rub each other up the wrong way. When this is the case, you need to learn how to manage your boss to remove whatever is getting in the way of the perfect relationship.

The first thing you need to do is to get inside your boss's head. If you don't understand what makes them tick, you can't hope to understand how to manage them. Part of this includes understanding the pressures they are under, so you also need to learn about your boss's boss – what makes *them* tick and how they relate to your boss.

Once you've identified what's going on from your boss's perspective, you need to look at your own position. When you run into problems with your boss, is it always because they are difficult, or might it sometimes be that you are unwittingly contributing to the problem? Once you've identified any shortcomings in yourself, you can address them.

Every boss is different, but there are certain skills you need in order to manage any boss successfully. Some of them you need to use constantly – such as assertiveness and good listening – while others you will need only occasionally, such as handling your own emotions when they run high, or addressing tricky topics with your boss without causing confrontation.

And then, of course, there are the problem bosses. Maybe they are only a problem some of the time, but there's no denying that certain bosses have some unsavoury characteristics, from throwing tantrums to putting you down in public. If your boss exhibits any of these unfortunate traits, you need to know how to set about eliminating the problem.

How to Manage Your Boss tells you everything you need to know to ensure your relationship with your boss is a long and happy one. And when the success of your relationship leads to promotion and new challenges, you'll have all the skills you need to manage the next boss, and the next one.

The final step will be to make sure each member of your team (if you have one) reads this book, not only to show what an enlightened boss you are, but also to make sure that you have a team which is as easy, enjoyable and rewarding to manage as you deserve.

I

Knowing your boss

If you want a first class relationship with your boss, you have to start by getting to know them. You need to learn what makes them tick and, to understand the pressures on them, you also have to understand what makes *their* boss tick. Only once you understand what you're dealing with can you go on to look at the relationship between the two of you. Then you can really get on with managing the boss and creating the perfect working relationship.

CHAPTER 1

Understanding your boss

A good relationship with your boss is more important for you than it is for them. You have more to lose from a poor relationship than they have. And on top of that, you have only one immediate boss (or maybe two), while they almost certainly have more than just you in their team. So you're going to have to make the running here.

Your first step is to get to know your boss. I don't mean socially – I mean you need to be able to see the relationship from your boss's perspective. You need to know how they operate and what is important to them at work. To do this, you need to answer certain questions:

- What does the boss actually do?
- What sort of boss are they?
- What are their strengths and weaknesses?
- How does your boss communicate?
- What motivates your boss?
- What stresses your boss?

You can answer these questions easily with a bit of thought – they're not going to take you weeks of research. Even if you or the boss are new to the job, you can still find out what you don't know with a bit of observation and perhaps a few strategic questions to your colleagues. Let's have a look at each question in turn to see exactly what you're trying to determine.

What does the boss actually do?

Your job is to help the boss achieve their objectives. They probably have wider-ranging objectives than you, and you are responsible for only a part of what they hold responsibility for. For example, they may be responsible for sales throughout the country, while you are responsible only for sales in the south-west region. Or they may manage the entire accounts department, while you deal only with bought ledger.

So identify your boss's objectives. For example, their job may be to boost positive PR coverage for the whole organisation, or to ensure a smooth and cost-effective despatch system for all goods sent out to customers. Whatever their precise function, it's likely to be more comprehensive and to have more impact on the organisation than yours.

The point of this exercise is two-fold. That is to say, it will help you to understand:

- how much greater your boss's responsibilities are than your own. This helps you to put their relationship with you in perspective. Much as they may want a strong relationship with each of their team members, you may be a much smaller part of their working life than they are of yours

- the scope you have to be of more value to your boss. While your top priority is to meet the objectives in your job description, the most valuable team members are the ones who can give their boss support wherever it's needed. Without treading on your colleagues' toes, you can still increase your value to your boss by being able to step in when they need support elsewhere, because you understand the priorities and issues for the whole department, not just your own part of it.

The big picture

Once you understand your boss's objectives it makes it far easier for you to see the bigger picture that they have to look at every day. This means you can present ideas and solutions that meet all your boss's requirements, not only your own. For example, when they ask for ways to reduce costly accounting mistakes, you can come up with a proposal that works not only for bought ledger but also for customer accounts. This is more useful to your boss and, obviously, scores you more brownie points too.

Here are a few more questions to ask yourself; the answers will help you to understand your boss's job better, and how you fit into it:

- How many people does your boss manage in addition to you?
- How many people is your boss answerable to, and who are they?
- How much of your boss's time is spent simply managing the department (running team briefings, training, handling staff-related paperwork, communicating, holding interviews and appraisals and so on)?
- How much of your boss's time is spent generating and promoting ideas?
- What sort of decisions does your boss have to take?

By the time you've answered all these questions, you should have a good picture of the tasks and concerns that occupy your boss's attention. And you will be able to see that while a good relationship with you will make their life vastly easier, they don't have as much time as you to invest in it, and they have wider concerns than yours.

What sort of boss have you got?

There are lots of different types of boss and, while some are certainly better than others, many are neither good nor bad, except perhaps in

You need to identify your boss's working style so you can do your best to fit in with it.

relation to you. We all have our own working style – some of us like detailed work, some hate risk-taking, some are intuitive decision-makers and so on. You need to identify your boss's working style so you can do your best to fit in with it. Here are a few examples of types of working style – your boss may exhibit several of them.

- *Bureaucratic:* this boss sticks to the rules, and likes paperwork. They're not great risk-takers. *To keep them happy:* you need to put things in writing and stick to the rules yourself. Don't bother putting forward any proposals which involve taking major risks.

- *Laid back:* results are more important to this boss than dotting i's and crossing t's. So long as things are going well, they won't be too concerned with details. *To keep them happy:* don't bother them with petty details, just focus on getting the results they want.

- *Consultative:* if you have this kind of boss, they are likely to involve you in decisions, projects and information, and keep you in the loop generally. *To keep them happy:* don't be secretive around them. They won't necessarily want to be bothered with every detail of what you're up to, but they will want to feel that your general approach is as open as theirs.

- *Non-consultative:* quite the reverse, this boss never tells you what's going on until they decide that you need to know. While their judgement may often be right (if frustrating), sometimes you need to know more than they realise. *To keep them happy:* don't ask for information you don't require. If you do need to know something, explain why, so they realise your need to know.

- *Concerned with detail:* this is not necessarily the same as being bureaucratic, although it often goes alongside it. This boss will breathe down your neck most of the time if they can, always wanting to know the nitty-gritty of what you're doing and why. *To keep them happy:* give them plenty of progress reports and supply all the detail they want. This will make them feel they can trust you.

- *Focused on the big picture:* this boss doesn't want to be hassled with minor detail. They are concerned with objectives and results, and how they are achieved is your concern, not theirs. *To keep them happy:* don't trouble them with small things – use your initiative. Express ideas and suggestions in terms of the objectives and results that interest this boss.

Learn the lingo

Whether your boss's personal style is included in this list or not, you'll see that it's not hard to recognise how to keep your boss happy once you've identified their working style. Remember, this is really about how you work in relation to your boss, not how you work when you're left alone. Your boss may, in fact, have given you the job because you're different to them – an unorganised boss might have chosen an organised team member to look after the tasks they're not cut out for. But when you deal directly with them, it still helps if you can speak their language.

- *Creative:* originality and inventiveness are what grab this boss, and they want ideas and creative suggestions from you about everything from how to double sales to a novel approach to the Christmas party. *To keep them happy:* learn from them – and from other sources such as books – how to exercise your creative mind so you can approach problems and challenges in the same way they do.

- *Logical:* this boss likes all ideas and suggestions to be based on logical reasoning, not on creative leaps of the imagination. Facts and figures should back up every argument. *To keep them happy:* make sure you have data to justify every proposal or solution you bring to them.

- *Organised:* a tidy desk and a well-kept planner or diary are the hallmarks of this boss. They like plenty of lists, and they always know what their priorities are, both short- and long-term. *To keep them happy:* look organised yourself. This boss won't believe you can work effectively if your desk is a mess and you're always late for meetings.

- *Unorganised:* this boss may work very effectively, but they don't look it. Papers all over the place, always wondering where they're supposed to be next, and never quite appearing to be on top of the job. *To keep them happy:* learn to anticipate what they will want, because they won't. Give them plenty of warnings and reminders before deadlines or important meetings, but don't give the impression you're nannying them (unless you know they like it).

- *Proactive:* new projects get this boss excited, and they're always looking to initiate schemes and ideas. *To keep them happy:* show enthusiasm for their ideas, and be ready with plenty of your own, geared towards key objectives (yours and your boss's).

- *Reactive:* this boss spends more time responding to issues and ideas than initiating new ones. So they tend to be more thoughtful and less inclined to take risks (it's not unusual for them also to be the bureaucratic type). *To keep them happy:* don't try to get them to launch endless new projects. Instead, concentrate on getting the job done thoroughly and seeing things through to completion.

Bosses come in all shapes and sizes, and there's no one perfect type of boss (and no single version of the boss from hell, either). Here is a questionnaire to give you an idea of the kind of boss you're dealing with.

1. The plans for the new product launch were finalised at the end of last week, but you've just had a brilliant idea which will get the company lots of positive media interest. You grab five minutes with your boss to tell them about it. Do they:
    a) Tell you it's too late now; all the plans are fixed?
    b) Say they'll consider it if you give them a full written proposal by tomorrow morning?
    c) Recognise the quality of the idea and set about adjusting the plans to incorporate it?

2. You're concerned that the forms sent through by accounts have been filled out wrongly. You go to your boss and express your worries. Do they:
    a) Tell you to stop worrying, so long as the information you need is in there somewhere?
    b) Suggest you go and talk to accounts yourself and straighten it out?
    c) Pick up the pile of forms and storm off to the accounts department with them?

3. There's a possibility that your department may be relocated to a different part of the building in the next few months. Does your boss:
    a) Tell you this plan is in the offing and ask for your views on it while there's still time to feed them into the decision-making process?
    b) Wait until the plans are well under way and then let you know what's going on?
    c) Spring it on you a couple of weeks beforehand that you'll be moving?

4. You put in a proposal to the board a month ago for a new sales initiative. Senior managers – including your boss – are discussing it this morning. Does your boss:

a) Say nothing about it until you ask, and then simply inform you that no decision has been made yet?

b) Give you a brief outline of what was discussed?

c) Ask for you to be present at the relevant part of the meeting so that you can be involved in the discussions and answer any questions?

5. Your boss asked you to put together some research material for them over the next week. While you're doing this, do they:

a) Check how you're getting on several times a day, ask to see lists of organisations and websites you're checking out, and make frequent suggestions as to where else to go and what information to look for?

b) Ask you each day how you're getting on, and have a quick look over what you've done already?

c) Leave you well alone?

6. You're starting to suspect that one of your suppliers is putting their rates up faster than necessary. You go to your boss who:

a) Tells you it's up to you to solve the problem however you feel is best?

b) Suggests you phone round for a couple more quotes and then decide whether you'd be better off with another supplier?

c) Asks you to put together some figures so they can go through them?

7. Your boss is concerned that the latest team project is looking a bit stale, and needs a boost. Do they:

a) Hold a team session somewhere offbeat – the park or the local tenpin bowling alley – for a day of quirky idea-generating exercises?

b) Call everyone to the meeting room for an hour's brainstorming?

   c) Ask everyone to submit a brief written outline of suggestions for boosting the project's results?

8. You've realised that you could halve your delivery times without adding to the costs simply by changing your packaging material to a new, lightweight product you've sourced. You take the suggestion to your boss. Do they:

   a) Ask you to put together detailed figures on costs, package weights and delivery options?

   b) Suggest that you write them a one-page outline of what you're proposing with a few sample costings?

   c) Get as excited as you and start looking at samples straight away?

9. You ask your boss if you can take the day off on 6 August (three months away), for your sister's wedding. Does your boss:

   a) Open their diary, turn to the year planner section and study it in detail alongside their list headed 'Holiday Dates' before giving you an answer?

   b) Ask you to send them a quick memo so they have the request in writing?

   c) Tell you straight away they're sure that's fine – they'll worry about arranging cover later?

10. You need some information from a report which you lent to your boss. You go to their office and ask for it back. Do they:

   a) Look slightly panicky, rummage through several piles of papers on their desk, and then say they're very busy and they'll let you know when they've had a chance to track it down?

   b) Ask for five minutes, and then bring it in to you 20 minutes later?

   c) Reach into their filing cabinet or in-tray and pull the report out for you instantly?

11. It's the end of February and everyone is very busy and feeling a bit jaded. Does your boss:
    a) Boost everyone's moral by launching yet another exciting new project, despite the fact that several projects are under way already?
    b) Get the team together to discuss ways of breathing new life and energy into some of the projects you're already working on?
    c) Try to generate a bit more enthusiasm by jollying people along and taking the team out for a lunchtime drink?

12. You and a couple of colleagues have come up with an idea for boosting output. Does your boss:
    a) Tell you there's a lot going on in the department at the moment, and any new ideas should wait until things are quieter?
    b) Ask you to put your proposal in writing so they can have a look at it when they get a chance?
    c) Leap at the idea and get to work on it immediately?

If you answered *a* to any of these:

Your boss is clearly a strong example of their type, and will need the right handling. Identify your boss from the list opposite, and then look up how to keep them happy.

If you answered *b*:

Your boss has a tendency to the type identified in the list opposite, although it's not their dominant style. Nevertheless, it's worth checking out how to handle them.

If you answered *c*:

This is definitely not your boss's style.

Question number	Type of boss	See page ...
1	Bureaucratic	6
2	Laid back	6
3	Consultative	6
4	Non-consultative	6
5	Concerned with detail	6
6	Focused on the big picture	7
7	Creative	7
8	Logical	7
9	Organised	8
10	Unorganised	8
11	Proactive	8
12	Reactive	8

When you analyse your boss, you may well identify other dominant traits which you need to adapt to in order to develop a good working relationship. Once you've established what sort of boss you have, you will be able to answer two more important questions:

- What impresses your boss?
- What winds your boss up?

The answers to these questions will doubtless relate to their work style. For example, a stickler for detail is likely to be wound up by slap-dash work. But think through your experiences of your boss, and your team mates' experiences, and draw up a list of things you have known your boss respond particularly well or badly to. For example:

Impressed	Irritated
Putting forward ideas without being asked	Lateness
Offering to stay late to complete a project	Timewasting
Using initiative	Asking for approval for every little task
Bringing in outsiders to help with projects	Bringing them problems
Finding solutions to problems on your own	Complaining

This exercise should give you a good picture of how your boss likes *you* to work. The boss in the example above clearly wants to see evidence of commitment, and for you to think for yourself and act independently. They don't like negativity, lack of professionalism or people who can't use their initiative. This information is a huge boost to your campaign to manage your boss effectively.

What are your boss's strengths and weaknesses?

Next, you need to identify what your boss's strengths and weaknesses are, both in their work style and in the way they handle you and other people. Once you know this, you will have a better idea of where your boss needs support, or where you will need to make allowances. After all, your boss is only human, and none of us is perfect. Your boss has to be allowed a few flaws and weaknesses, and it's up to you to be able to manage them.

Recognising your boss's strengths is also useful. These are areas where you can relax, as well as learn from your boss's example. While strengths are essentially positive for you as well as the boss, some bosses are very sensitive about any criticism – direct or implied – in areas where they feel confident of their abilities. So don't give the impression you're trying to tell your boss how to do something that they already do well.

Here are a few questions to answer, to help you identify your boss's strong and weak points:

- How do you and your team mates feel about your boss? What do you like most and least about them?

- How popular is your boss among colleagues outside the department?

- How well does your boss handle people who make mistakes?

- Is your boss prone to emotional displays? If so, which emotions do they show most often, and are these negative (such as impatience) or positive (such as enthusiasm)?

- Does your boss get the best from you? If not, how could they get more from you?

- What part of their job would you say your boss was best at?

- What part of the job are they weakest at?

- How close does your boss come to meeting the objectives of the department?

- Is your boss good at making decisions?

- Is your boss supportive of you and the rest of the team?

How does your boss communicate?

Communication is essential to any manager's job, and it will help you to understand your boss's personal style. In particular, you need to analyse their level of openness, and their ability to put information across.

As far as openness is concerned, consider how readily your boss passes on information to you. Some bosses tell their team everything they can,

Some bosses tell their team everything they can, and others are naturally highly secretive.

and others are naturally highly secretive. But most are somewhere between the two, having certain types of information they tend to with-hold or pass on, and not others. For example:

- background information about current projects
- information from other departments
- information from senior management
- confidential information
- information about customers
- information about competitors.

Many bosses will be very open with some of these categories but not with others.

Once you've identified the areas where your boss is open – and not so open – you can get a picture of what determines their openness. Maybe they don't give information because they don't realise you need it. Or perhaps they're worried they'll get into trouble with management or colleagues. Or maybe they don't trust you to keep confidential infor-mation that way. Or perhaps they think you wouldn't understand the implications of certain types of information.

Once you can see the picture, you can start to manage your boss to be more open with you by working on building their trust in you, or by explaining why it would help to have certain information.

Matter of choice

How does your boss generally prefer to communicate with you: phone, face-to-face, email, memo? Whatever their preference is, it will help them – and therefore you – if you use the same method. So if they send you an email, reply by email. If they'd wanted to talk to you face-to-face or on the phone they'd have done so. Respect their choice. Equally, if they always pick up the phone when they want to contact you, opt for the phone yourself when you want to communicate with them. Obviously there will be times when there is a particular reason for choosing a different means of communication, but default at using their preferred method.

When it actually comes to imparting information, some bosses are very good at it, while others are hopeless at explaining things so they make sense. If your boss falls into this category, you're going to have to do some work yourself to make sure there are no crucial lapses of communication. If you don't understand instructions or briefings, you could be in trouble, and your boss will insist they explained everything clearly to you…so it must be your fault.

If your boss is poor at communicating information clearly, the solution is two-fold:

- Keep asking questions until you have the information you need. Don't be afraid to say, 'I don't quite understand why this is being handed over to our department' (or whatever). It's far better to say that you don't understand than to keep quiet and then make mistakes later.

- Put your understanding of the information, the brief or the instructions in writing and email it to your boss saying, 'This is just to confirm the brief for the report on the results of the recent PR campaign.' That way, if you've got anything wrong, the onus is on your boss to correct it now before it matters.

What motivates your boss?

All bosses want to see results, but there are plenty of other factors which make them feel more or less motivated during their working day. For instance:

- a convivial working atmosphere

- a feeling of being in control

- challenge

- a sense of order

- a relaxed atmosphere

- positive attitudes

- good relations with other people

- competition – perhaps with other organisations, or with their own track record, or with colleagues.

Your boss needs to be motivated to enjoy their job just as you do, and often you can help with this. If they like to be surrounded by enthusiasm, or enjoy feeling that tasks are being carried out methodically, or simply want to have time for a good meal in the middle of the day, you can often provide, or help to accommodate, these things.

What stresses your boss?

Just as it helps to know what motivates your boss, so it is clearly useful to know what stresses them. The more you can work to 'reduce their stress levels, the better your relationship with them will be. So compile a list of the things that most get up your boss's nose. Here are some possibilities to get you started:

- time pressure

- pressure from senior management

- problems

- a noisy atmosphere

- negativity

- not being consulted by team members

- being bothered with what they see as petty details

- lack of organisation

- conflict.

Cut the boss's stress levels

Try compiling a list of the three traits you exhibit which you reckon most irritate or stress your boss. Be honest. They may not be bad characteristics in themselves, just ones which rile your boss. Perhaps you work more slowly than they'd like, or you're very talkative, or you don't always double check your facts. Whatever three traits you pick, make a conscious effort to minimise them around your boss, and see what a difference it makes.

What pressures is your boss under?

Your work and your mood is affected by your boss, so it stands to reason that they are influenced by *their* boss – their mood, their attitude, the demands they make. You can't hope to get to grips with your own boss unless you also examine this relationship.

You can start by conducting the same kind of analysis of your boss's boss as you have just done for your own. Answer the questions:

- What does your boss's boss actually do?

- What sort of boss are they?

- What are their strengths and weaknesses?

- How does your boss's boss communicate?

- What motivates them?

- What stresses them?

If you don't know your boss's boss as well as your own, your answers may be a little skimpier, but that's OK – you're at one remove from this boss. You should still be able to get a clear enough picture to understand what pressures your boss is under, and where they are well supported.

Having gone through this process, you can flesh out the picture more by analysing a couple more points:

- How good does the relationship between your boss and their boss appear?

- What are the main areas of friction?

Appearances aren't everything, but if the relationship is particularly strong or weak, it will show. If you can identify the main areas of friction, this will indicate where your boss feels most under pressure – when their own views or style are contradicted by the directions that come down to them.

You also need to consider the company culture as a whole. It is very difficult – indeed often impossible – for your boss to operate counter to the prevailing culture. If the organisation is highly competitive, they will have to be competitive to survive. If their boss, senior management and the organisation as a whole has little regard for staff welfare, your boss is going to find it impossible to put staff welfare at the top of their

Look at your boss's prevailing attitudes in the light of the corporate culture, and you will often see a pattern.

priority list. Every policy or action that requires approval from above will be rejected.

Look at your boss's prevailing attitudes in the light of the corporate culture, and you will often see a pattern. This is not to say that any negative attitudes on your boss's part are blameless – after all, they chose to work in this culture. (But then, so did you.) Nevertheless, attitudes which are backed up by the organisation as a whole are much harder to shift, and you need to recognise this. If your boss does try to break away from the norm, they will put themselves under great pressure, and will need all the support they can get.

Building the picture

Now you have consciously considered how your boss works, and what makes them tick, you have the information you need to build a strong working relationship. All this information tells you how they like people to interact with them. For example:

- If you've established that they are a stickler for detail, you'll need to make sure you give them detailed data and progress reports.

- If they hate anything that smacks to them of lack of professionalism, you'll need to make sure you present work neatly, turn up on time and don't criticise the customers in front of them.

- If one of their weak points is a short temper, you'll want to avoid winding them up, and brush up on your skills for handling anger or tantrums.

- If they are motivated by status, show them you respect their seniority, and sell them ideas by concentrating on what a successful outcome would do for their reputation.

- If your boss is easily stressed by time pressure, always deliver work early and do what you can to ease time pressure for them.

- If your boss is poor at communicating background information, learn to ask the right questions and let them know why you're asking. For instance, 'Can you tell me why the board wants this information? It will help me focus my research on the things that matter most to them.'

- If your boss is under pressure from their own boss, they will need a great deal of back-up and support from you to resist it. Don't simply put equal and opposite pressure on them – help them find a solution that keeps everyone happy.

All this should give you a clear picture of why you need to understand your boss in order to build a good relationship with them. The more you know about them, the better you can target your own skills and style to mesh snugly with theirs. And that's the key to managing your boss.

Are you part of the problem or part of the solution?

If you look around at your colleagues in your team and in neighbouring departments, you're bound to see that some have better relationships with their boss than others. And often you can see why: many people have only themselves to blame. Of course, in some cases any short-comings are clearly down to a tricky boss. But even so, some people handle the same boss better than others do.

Now turn the spotlight on yourself. Is it possible that you are one of those who isn't doing as much as you could to develop the best possible relationship with the boss? Very few of us create frequent major problems in the way we deal with our boss, but most of us cause occasional difficulties, or simply miss opportunities to make the relationship even better than it is.

This isn't, of course, a deliberate act. We don't realise that we are contributing to the problem. The answer is to analyse our behaviour, and to see how we can adapt it to avoid problems with the boss. (Chapter 5 covers the third step – creating positive opportunities.)

There are certain skills we need to address which are important with any boss – skills which are guaranteed to make you an easier, more effective and more rewarding member of the team from your boss's point of view:

- building your skill base
- improving your overall image
- managing your time effectively.

Let's take each of these skills in turn so you can see where there might be room for improvement.

> **No change there**
>
> Creating new skills, and finding ways to improve your relationship with your boss, is not about transmogrifying yourself into someone you're not. We can't change our personalities overnight, and it would be futile to try. It's all about bringing our best points to the fore and learning to control our less helpful tendencies so that we present the most effective and constructive side of ourselves.

Building your skill base

The better skilled you are to do your job, the more use you will be to the boss. It stands to reason. If you know how to enter bookings into the system when the person who normally does it is off sick, you'll be of more use than if you don't. So one of the first steps in showing the boss how dependable and useful you are, is to develop any skills which will make your boss's job easier.

Next time someone is unexpectedly off sick, or extra help is needed, or the team takes on a new project, your boss may be tempted to panic that there's no one with the skills to get the job done. But not with you around, they won't. They'll think of you and smile with relief: they can count on you to step into the breach.

So what sort of skills should you learn? Clearly you need to learn skills which will directly benefit the department and your boss. So it's a good idea to learn some of your colleagues' skills. This might mean mugging up on procedures, learning to use a particular piece of software, or perhaps getting a new skill under your belt such as giving presentations, writing reports or running training sessions. Or perhaps you could learn a foreign language (or brush up on one) if your department has started doing more overseas business.

The important thing is to make sure that whatever you choose to learn is genuinely useful to your boss. So don't bother learning Spanish if you've already got two fluent Spanish speakers in the department and almost no Spanish customers. Look instead for areas where under-staffing can be a problem – the sort of thing which leaves everyone in the lurch whenever Sarah goes on holiday, or Ali is off sick on the day of a big presentation.

And how are you going to acquire these extra skills? The best way to improve or learn any of these skills is to start by talking to your boss. Tell them you've noticed that Robin is often overworked and there's no one else with the skills to take on some of the load. Or that now Mandy has left, there's no one to provide holiday cover for Kieran. Explain that you'd like to learn these skills, and you want their opinion – would it be useful? And what's the best way to go about it?

If you're right about your boss's life being easier if you have these skills, they will be really pleased at your offer and will back you up with what-ever help you need.

Mind out for other people's toes

Your colleagues may get understandably edgy if you suddenly start trying to learn their jobs. They may worry that you're trying to oust them. So be diplomatic about it. Don't give the impression you want to take over and become the team's star presenter or researcher or software operator. Make it clear you simply want to be able to stand in or give support when staffing is stretched. If one of your colleagues is particularly territorial and touchy, it would be better to look for a new skill to learn that doesn't impinge at all on what they do.

If you've misjudged and a particular skill isn't going to help, they'll put you straight (in which case you can say, 'I'd like to make myself more useful to the team; what new skill could I learn that would be helpful?'). So approaching them is a sensible way to double check that you've picked the right skills.

Now you've picked the right skill to learn, and you've got your boss's support, things should be easy. It will make your boss's life much easier (which is what you want) if you have already prepared an idea or two for learning your new skills which you can present to them, asking for their support if you need it. For example:

- Ask them to enrol you on a course to learn to write press releases.
- Offer to stay late a few times to learn the new software, but ask them to make sure there's a terminal you can use.
- Ask to join in a training session that's already been scheduled, perhaps in another department.
- Offer to enrol on an evening course at your local college, but ask to leave 10 minutes early on a Tuesday in order to get there on time.

Your boss will clearly be more impressed the more effort you are prepared to put into adding this new skill to your portfolio. There's no point putting in extra hours if it's quite unnecessary, but offering to do an evening class or to work through lunch will clearly score you brownie points if it helps you learn the skill faster.

Just one word of caution here: make sure you don't bite off too much. Don't promise more than you can deliver.

Just one word of caution here: make sure you don't bite off too much. If you tell your boss you're going to learn to speak French and then give up before you've mastered *la plume de ma tante*, you'll end up looking worse in your boss's eyes than if you'd never started. Don't promise more than you can deliver.

ASSESSMENT TIME

Here are some ideas for assessing the most productive skills to learn:

- Write down a list of your team mates and identify an area where each of them could use support or back-up.
- Look around the department and see which skills are missing from the whole team.
- If anyone has left the department – or is planning to – consider whether this leaves any skills gaps.

Be honest about your own abilities:

- Pick a skill (or a few skills) which you feel sure you are capable of acquiring.
- Make sure you'll be able to practise or remember the skill until you're called on to do it for real.
- Don't offer to learn a skill which you don't have the time or self-discipline to learn.
- Pick a skill which you feel motivated to learn and will enjoy.

Improving your overall image

Have you noticed how some people come across as being naturally successful and positive, a real bonus to have around? While others seem to be natural losers, weak personalities? In fact, some of the former group are not more successful or useful than their colleagues, and many of the latter category are skilled at their jobs and an asset to their team. But it's as important to come across as being an asset as it is actually to be one.

The point about these two extremes is that the first type – those who appear successful and positive – are the ones people want around. And that includes your boss. Your boss may know their team well enough to recognise the strengths of those who seem at first glance to be losers, but they would still rather have the strengths *and* the positive image. So if you want to develop the best possible relationship with your boss, you need to cultivate the best possible image.

Various factors go to build up the image you project:

- appearance
- confidence
- energy
- positive attitude
- likeableness
- trustworthiness.

Appearance

If you look smart and professional, people will assume you are smart and professional. This doesn't mean wearing a pinstripe suit if your company dress code is informal, but it does mean making sure your clothes are clean, fresh and as smart as anyone else's.

As a general guide, dress in the same sort of way as your boss. If they dress casually, be casual yourself. If they go for a smart style, you follow suit (if you'll forgive the pun). This helps to create an empathy between you, and encourages your boss to feel that you're their sort of person. This doesn't mean you have to follow the same fashions as them – simply match their level of smartness.

Be consistent

It's essential to be consistent in your image. It's no good turning up at work looking well groomed almost every day, but turning up looking crumpled once every couple of weeks or so. You will simply undo all the good work of those other days when you made the effort. It's the untypical appearance which will be most noticeable and stick in people's memories – and that may be the day the MD turns up in the office, or a key customer calls in.

Body language is also key to using your appearance to project the right image. We can't change our appearance completely but, with practice, we can make a few simple changes which will have a significant effect:

- Stand up straight (not stiffly to attention, but not slouching either).
- Look ahead (not at the floor).
- Make eye contact with whoever you're talking to.
- Use open gestures with your arms relaxed – don't use defensive, closed gestures such as crossed arms and legs.
- When sitting, sit well back in the chair rather than perching on the edge.

If your posture and body language leaves room for improvement, practise these changes in front of a mirror and see what a difference they make. If you are aware of your body language as much as possible, and adapt it to follow these guidelines, you'll find it won't be long before the improved version becomes natural to you.

Confidence

If you project confidence, people will assume you are capable. If you tend to say things like, 'Ooh, I'm not sure I can do that' they will doubt your ability, even if you can actually do the thing very well. So being confident doesn't mean blowing your own trumpet, it simply means saying 'Yes, I can' instead of 'I don't know if I can'.

This kind of confidence not only gives a better impression of your abilities, it also reassures your boss, or whoever you're talking to. They will feel far happier about handing over a task to someone who says confidently that they can handle it, rather than someone who says they're not sure. That's why your boss wants confident people around them – it takes a load off their mind.

If you really aren't confident that you can do something, trust your boss. They wouldn't delegate a task to you if they didn't think you could do it. So give a confident reply even if you want support. For example: 'That sounds like a challenge. So long as I get the support I need, I'm sure I can do that.'

Energy

Are you a dynamic, impressive personality? If not, would you like to be? These are the kind of people who are great to have around, and you can be one of them. That will make your boss feel they've got a real asset on their team. You can give an impression of far greater energy just by incorporating a few simple techniques into your repertoire. As with improving your posture and body language, just practise until they become natural:

- Speak clearly without mumbling.

- Greet people with a smile.

- Be ready with a firm handshake.

- Sound interested in what you are saying and in what others are saying (there's more about listening skills in Chapter 8).

- Don't rush around, but move and speak at an upbeat pace.

Signs of life

Have a look around you. You'll see some people who always look full of energy and seem like positive powerhouses of activity. Others come across as weak, listless, mousy or just plain dozy. Their level of achievement doesn't necessarily reflect this image, but the impression they give seems to count for more than what they actually do. Try to identify what it is about people at the extremes of each category that gives the impression it does. Often it may be their appearance, their tone of voice, or the way they move.

Positive attitude

Many of us are natural optimists and have no problem on this score. But some of us find it hard to be positive and enthusiastic about everything. We're too worried that things aren't that rosy, and the optimists are kidding themselves. We feel it's our duty to keep everyone's feet on the ground.

Trouble is, most people – bosses included – find it frustrating and depressing being around someone who seems to be negative all the time. You may think you're a realist, but they may see you as more of a harbinger of doom. If this problem seems intractable, it's not. It's all a matter of presentation.

The fact is that people like you are important. You *do* keep everyone else's feet on the ground, and often you point out potential problems no one else was addressing. So don't stop. You simply need to couch it in terms that sound positive. So instead of focusing exclusively on the negative, present a more rounded view. If the team is discussing the proposal for a new product launch, resist the temptation to say, 'It'll be a disaster'. Say something like, 'It's a great idea, and I love the sound of the special effects. I'm just concerned that we haven't got the time or resources to prepare something on this scale and really carry it off.'

You've made your point, but in a positive way. Rather than a sweeping rejection of the proposal, you've made a constructive and useful contribution. You've followed the three rules for making a negative point appear positive:

1. Make your remarks specific (not, 'It won't work' but, 'We haven't the time and resources to prepare something on this scale and really carry it off.')

2. Always add a positive remark to counter the negativity ('It's a great idea, and I love the sound of the special effects.')

3. Use mild language, rather than dismissive or negative terms (not, 'It won't work,' or, 'It's a major problem,' but rather, 'I'm concerned,' or 'My one worry is…').

Likeableness

Your boss wants people around them they like and enjoy spending time with. A good personal relationship does wonders for your professional relationship – the two are closely interlinked. What's more, however well you manage your boss, there will always be times when things don't go as planned. Your boss will be far more understanding and forgiving if they like you than if they don't.

Your boss wants people around them they like and enjoy spending time with. A good personal relationship does wonders for your professional relationship.

There are a few basic characteristics which have a huge impact on how much people like you. Here's a quick checklist – mark yourself out of five on each point, and be honest:

Characteristic	Score (1=low, 5=high)
You show an interest in other people	
You are a good listener	
You use your sense of humour, but never against your boss or your team mates	
You don't gossip behind people's backs	
You aren't arrogant	
You don't put people down	

24–30: You're obviously a likeable person, whom everyone in the team gets along well with

18–23: You doubtless have friends in your team, but there is scope for you to become more popular with your colleagues and your boss

12–17: You'll do yourself no favours in your relationship with your team mates or your boss unless you work harder on being likeable

6–11: Whoops. You're not teacher's pet, are you? Still, compensate yourself with a bonus mark for honesty, and get to work on becoming more popular with the boss.

And remember, your boss isn't blind, and if you exhibit unlikeable characteristics towards other people it will influence their view of you. If you belittle junior members of the team it will do you no favours in your boss's eyes, even if you don't direct it at them personally.

Trustworthiness

Your boss will have far more respect for you, and confidence in you, if they know they can trust you. This means making sure you never break a confidence and can be trusted to keep a secret. Just because the boss didn't specifically swear you to secrecy, doesn't mean that you're necessarily free to start gossiping. There are times when it is clear that your boss wants information kept private, and they will want to know that you can identify these times for yourself without needing it spelt out for you.

Trust is also about doing what you say you will. If your boss gives you a task to do, it's important to see it through and not let them down. Once they know they can rely on you, especially when a task is urgent or very important, it will do your relationship no end of good.

ASSESSMENT TIME

Answer the following questions honestly in order to assess your personal image and identify areas for improvement:

- Are you always smartly dressed and well groomed?
- Is your body language and posture as good as it might be?
- Do you rise to a challenge with confidence, or do you express doubts in your own ability?
- Do you project an impression of energy? If not, what characteristics are holding you back?
- Do you express negative views in negative terms? Do you make broad generalisations such as 'It won't work'?
- How well did you score on the likeability guide? Is there any room for improvement?
- Have you ever betrayed your boss's trust, even over small matters?

Use the answers to these questions to draw up a list of areas where you can improve your overall image.

Managing your time effectively

Your boss isn't going to be happy if you're in the habit of missing meetings or delivering work late. Even if you are on time, cutting things fine does nothing to inspire the boss with confidence in you. If, on the other hand, you're always on top of your workload, usually available to help out with urgent, last-minute tasks, and you always turn up on time, your boss will see you as reliable, professional and exactly the kind of person they need on their team.

It's all about time management. Most of us are passable at this skill: even when we feel or appear useless at it, most tasks are completed by the deadline and we're not too late very often. However, few of us are entirely without failings. Perhaps we get things done, but only after generating an air of panic and frenetic activity around ourselves, or becoming irritable and snappy as we see the deadline looming. Or perhaps we're generally organised, but an unexpected delay throws us out entirely. Or we get the job done, but sometimes have to compromise on quality. Or our lack of organisation creates problems for other people, as we forget to pass on tasks or information until the last minute, or have to be nagged to fulfil our promises.

There's almost always scope to improve your time-management skills, and doing so will make you an easier, more effective and more rewarding team member for your boss. So what do you have to do?

Clear 15 minutes a day

The first step to controlling how you spend your time is to create 15 minutes a day during which you can organise yourself. If you don't do this, you will spend all your time running to catch up with yourself. If your time management is poor, this can sound like a real Catch 22: you can't manage your time until you can spare 15 minutes a day, and you can't find 15 minutes a day until you have managed your time.

Yet that, I'm afraid, is the bottom line. However, the good news is that having cleared your 15 minutes a day, you'll get on top of the organisation process really fast, and find you're saving yourself far more than a quarter of an hour each day. So where will the 15 minutes come from? Here are a few suggestions:

- Arrive at work 15 minutes earlier each day and spend that first bit of time getting organised.

- Find time on the way to or from work if you can.

- Do it over breakfast before you leave home (a bit impractical if you have children, but easy if you breakfast alone).

- Stay a few minutes later at the office, and make it a rule that you won't leave until you've done it.

- If your home life allows it, allocate a few minutes each evening after you get home.

The important thing is to keep this time sacrosanct, and don't allow anything else to encroach on it. That's why quieter times of day – such as after everyone else has left the office – tend to be the easiest to stick to.

And the good news...

Actually, once you get into the swing of this time-management thing, you'll find that 15 minutes is generally the most you need. Often five minutes is all it takes – for a process that can save you massively more time.

Intelligence-gathering

Now you've cleared yourself time for organising, you'd better have something to organise. That's the next part. You need to spend your day collecting things to organise. Get yourself a notebook and pen, and never go anywhere without them. Take them to meetings, to lunch, even home on the train with you. In your notebook, you need to write down anything which crops up during the day and which requires any action, thought, checking up or information any time in the future. So you'll need to jot down (any note form will do so long as you can read it back accurately):

- every time you promise someone you'll call them back

- every time anyone else undertakes to contact you

- every meeting, appointment or event that is arranged

- every meeting or event that you need to know about, even if you don't need to be there (for example, you may need to know that sales are making a decision at Friday's meeting on which products to push this month)

- every action point that occurs to you or that anyone passes on to you (this is why you need the notebook with you on the way home from work, especially for that moment when you suddenly think, 'I must get a copy of that new book on handling software crashes when it comes out').

Keep a folder with your notebook so that if you acquire this kind of information in an email or memo, or handed to you on a Post-it note, you can store it without having to copy it into your notebook. Within a matter of days you'll get so into the habit of doing this that you won't even notice the process. But you will feel fully in control – everything you need to know is stored in that single notebook or its accompanying folder.

By the way, trust no one. If someone says they'll call you back, write it down anyway. Otherwise, when they forget, you'll have no mechanism for picking up the error. If you have a note that you're expecting a call back by Wednesday, you can do something about it if the call doesn't materialise.

Trust no one. If someone says they'll call you back, write it down anyway.

> ### Keep it together
>
> The only thing you must remember is to keep the notebook and folder with you all the time. If you don't, you'll find yourself with notes and jottings all over the place and you'll be back where you started – disorganised.

Manage your diary

You are now ready to spend 15 minutes (ish) a day transferring all this information to your diary. Well, almost ready. First you need a decent diary, so go and get one if you don't already have one. Your diary needs to be big enough to break each day down by time, and have plenty of room each day for notes as well. OK, now we can start.

All you need to do now is to copy across everything from your notebook and folder into your diary. So, for example:

- If you told someone you'd call them back on Monday, jot it down under Monday's notes. If you said you'd call them specifically at 2.30 on Monday, put it down in the diary section (rather than notes) at 2.30. You might find it helpful to add the phone number too.

- If you have a leaflet in your folder about an event you need to attend, enter it in your diary under the relevant date, along with any other information or phone number that goes with it.

- If you make an appointment to visit somewhere, put it in your diary. Under the daily notes, include directions for getting there if you need them, and the phone number.

- If someone said they'd call you back by the end of the week, make a note for Friday or Monday morning to chase them if you haven't heard by then. If you have, you can simply ignore the note when you come to it.

- If you made yourself an action point to get prices from a supplier, for example, find a convenient slot in your diary for doing it and write it down on the to-do list for that day.

- Obviously you will also add any meetings to the diary, and include any special notes of anything you need to remember to take with you.

As you get used to the system, you will probably find that you enter many things directly into your diary rather than into the notebook. But you'll still need the notebook because some of your notes will tell you to do something you need to think about the best time for – and you don't always have time for this process until later.

That's your daily diary time – 15 minutes should be ample each day. On top of this, you will also need to spend time with your diary at the start of each year, month and week. Here's what you need to do:

Yearly planning

This will take around half an hour, and should be done just before the start of each new year. Enter all the dates you already have for the year ahead:

- special events such as trade shows
- regular meetings
- regular events such as a monthly department lunch
- holidays
- personal time off (for anniversaries, children's birthdays or anything else you want to keep free)
- allocate 15 minutes at the start of each month for a similar diary session.

New leaf

If you're turning over a new leaf and investing in a new diary now, you'll need to do your yearly planning straight away for the rest of this year, and do all the monthly planning for the rest of this month, along with the weekly planning for the remainder of the week. Then you're ready to start using the diary daily.

Monthly planning

This is the time to schedule in blocks of time for projects which need time set aside but aren't specific timed events. For example:

- writing proposals or reports
- doing research
- preparing for presentations
- dealing with regular paperwork
- catching up with letter writing
- holding interviews (if you're a manager)

...and so on. Some of these may need several blocks of time set aside – perhaps short ones – while others may need a single day or half day.

Weekly planning

You should start each week with a few blank spaces in your diary, so before they get filled in with appointments and meetings, spend five minutes (on Friday afternoon or Monday morning) allocating any remaining tasks, such as:

- catching up with phone calls
- catching up with emails

- taking phone calls – if your time is very busy and you often field calls, you need time to reply to them all

- handling miscellaneous tasks – these are the ones which usually mess up your time. You don't know what they'll be, but you know extra tasks always crop up. So be smart and schedule time for them. An hour or two on Friday afternoons is usually good.

- delegating and monitoring work if you're a manager.

With your yearly, monthly and weekly planning in place, you can see how 15 minutes a day of adding ongoing tasks and information as they crop up will give you a diary which is more like a bible. Everything you need is in there.

Prioritise

There are lots of systems for prioritising work according to urgency and importance. In theory they work well, but in practice if you're really organising your time properly you shouldn't need them. The point is that if you don't get through everything on your list for the day, at least you'll have got through the tasks that matter most. However, you should be able to see that the logical result of this process is going to be a backlog that grows ever bigger.

The real answer is to make sure that you get through all the work each day. If you can't do this almost every day, you're taking on too much work or scheduling it unrealistically. If Thursday is already packed, don't add to it jobs that could just as well wait until Friday. If you never get through your work, offload or dump some of it, with your boss's approval if necessary.

The real answer is to make sure that you get through all the work each day.

Having said that, however, there are occasional days when havoc breaks loose and you don't get through your to-do list for the day. In case this happens, it's worth making yourself a note warning you if anything you mark in your diary particularly needs to be done on the day indicated no matter what else is happening. Any system that suits you is fine: mark the task with a highlighter pen, write it in red ink, or put an asterisk beside it.

ASSESSMENT TIME

How many of the following questions can you answer 'yes' to?

- Do you know exactly what your key objectives are?
- Do you spend most of your time on your top priorities?
- Do you set aside a period each day to organise your time?
- Do you keep an up-to-date diary?
- Does your diary (or some equivalent system) include a daily to-do list?
- Do you complete every task on time, or early?
- Do you arrive on time for every meeting and appointment?
- Do you work in relative calm, without last-minute panics?

If you answered 'no' to any of these, it will have highlighted an area where you could do more to plan and use your time more effectively.

CHAPTER 3

Developing specific skills

Now you've learnt the broad skills which you need in order to eliminate difficulties with your boss, what about the specific skills that apply to this particular boss? In Chapter 1, you identified what type of boss you have, their strengths and weaknesses, and what stresses and motivates them. Now you need to do much the same for yourself, to identify which aspects of your character are a positive bonus, and which may be holding you back.

However, in your boss's case you were making an assessment by broad objective measures. This time, you need to assess yourself *relative to your boss*. In other words, it's not a matter of finding your greatest strengths or weaknesses in the job overall, but the biggest factors when it comes to relating to your boss.

What are your strengths?

It may be that you consider your greatest strengths in the job to be, say, attention to detail and thoroughness. But these aren't necessarily your best points when it comes to relating to the boss. They could be a huge bonus if your boss needs someone with an eye for detail, but with some bosses these could even be weaknesses – if your boss is more interested in the bigger picture and is irritated by people who fulfil tasks more slowly than they would (even if you are doing them more thoroughly), such characteristics will rile them and certainly won't help your working relationship.

That doesn't mean you should discard these skills – they *are* strengths in the broader sense, and they may well be positive points with the next boss. The point is that this exercise entails looking for your strengths in managing this particular boss, not looking for your overall strengths.

So what you need to do is to identify the areas where your personality or work style is a positive boon to your relationship with your boss. Here are a few possibilities to give you an idea:

- You're very thick-skinned, which is a great bonus with a boss as irascible as yours.

- You're patient and tolerant when your boss is weak at communicating.

- You're thorough in your work, and your boss hates petty mistakes.

- You're creative, which your boss appreciates since they are not.

- You're good at resolving people problems; your boss isn't and likes to leave you to handle such problems or advise them on how to do so.

- You're very self-motivated, which is a big plus with a boss who does nothing to motivate the team.

- You're a good team-player, and your boss likes people who can work as a team.

- You like to concentrate on the big issues; your boss appreciates not being troubled with minor details.

- You're excellent at number work, so your boss can gratefully hand over that part of their job to you.

- You work well alone and use your initiative, so your boss can leave you to get on with tasks.

- Your work styles are similar in a way which helps you understand how each other thinks.

- You get on well together and enjoy each other's company.

**The reason you need to recognise your strengths
is so that you can capitalise on them.**

How many?

Try to identify at least two or three strengths – I'm sure you have at least that many. But if half a dozen spring to mind, list all of them. You're looking for strengths which you use fairly frequently, rather than ones which only rarely come into play.

These are just a few possible strengths – all of which relate directly to the boss concerned – to give you an idea of the kind of strengths you must identify in yourself. The reason you need to recognise your strengths is so that you can capitalise on them. Once you know what they are you can:

- hone them, to make them even more relevant and beneficial to your relationship with the boss

- make sure you exercise them whenever possible

- look for related abilities you can develop to add more value to the relationship – for example, if your boss regards you as a real asset because you're quick and able when it comes to computer skills, you can make a point of learning everything useful you can about any new software, and developing ways to use the existing software more effectively.

What are your weaknesses?

We've already seen how thoroughness and attention to detail, for example, can actually be weaknesses in relating to some bosses, despite being strengths with other bosses. So you need to examine the working relationship and see where your weaknesses lie with this particular boss. Again, here are a few ideas to get you started:

- You have a tendency to lose your rag with your boss when they rile you – which they frequently do.

- You're inclined to sulk when your boss gives you a hard time.

- You have little patience with your boss when they act more slowly than you'd like – and it shows.

- You're easily influenced by your emotions – when your boss gives you a hard time or things are going badly, your standard of work drops noticeably.

- You work fast, but not always as thoroughly as your boss would like.

- You work well alone, but you're not so good at working alongside others.

- You sometimes upset people by being blunt and speaking your mind – your boss often has to pick up the pieces.

- You tend to ask your boss for frequent guidance or approval, when they have other things to concentrate on and would prefer you to leave them alone.

- You're very verbose, and your boss would rather you kept your questions and contributions briefer.

- You're very untidy and, although you feel you work better that way, your boss feels otherwise.

- You are good at most of your job, but you've never really got the hang of keeping on top of the paperwork. Your boss considers orderly paperwork essential.

- You don't always refer decisions which you consider minor to your boss.

Life isn't fair...

You'll notice from the suggestions of possible weaknesses that some of them are only a response to provocative or unreasonable behaviour from the boss. If they didn't start it, you wouldn't have any cause to show your weakness. This may be true, but the exercise isn't about allocating blame, it's about improving your relationship with your boss. They're hardly likely to change, so if you want things to get better, you're going to have to be the one to make the changes, fair or not.

Once you've worked out where your natural behaviour or style are inhibiting a good relationship with your boss, you can take steps to improve things:

- Work on toning down or even removing those characteristics which get in the way of your working relationship (you'll find lots of tips later in this book to help you).

- Find other ways to achieve the same results without riling the boss. For example, suppose they don't like the way you double-check all the important figures because they think it takes too long. You, on the other hand, consider it vital (and you're probably right). Perhaps you could do the figurework – or at least the checking – when they're out of the office.

What motivates you?

It's helpful to identify what motivates you because if you feel demoralised and demotivated it's likely that your boss is failing to provide

If you feel demoralised it's likely that your boss is failing to provide whatever it is that you need to feel enthused and positive.

whatever it is that you need to feel enthused and positive. If you know what you need, you can do something about it, such as:

- talk to your boss and explain what you need

- find some way to generate the motivating factor yourself

- find some other motivating factor to drive you. Most of us are motivated by more than one thing, even if we have a prime motivator. If your main motivator is money, for example, but you can't extract a pay rise from your boss, perhaps you can concentrate on, say, the motivation of competing with colleagues or with your own track record.

So what motivates you? Opposite is a list of common motivating factors. In the middle column, mark down how available this form of motivation is in your job on a scale of 1–5. So if you are extremely well paid, score 5 next to money in the middle column. In the right-hand column award a mark from 1–5 according to how motivated you are by this particular factor. So if money isn't what motivates you in the least, score 1 in the right-hand column.

Obviously, the ideal job will give you an exact match between the middle and right-hand columns. Since almost no job is ideal, this isn't likely to happen, but it's not unrealistic to hope for an approximate match. What you really want to identify are any factors where the reality of the job differs significantly from your own personal motivations. These are the areas where you may be feeling dissatisfied and need to take action along the lines we have just looked at.

This exercise isn't going to tell you anything new and earth-shattering about yourself. The idea is to bring consciously to the fore any motivational problems which you have not addressed before, so that you can do something about them.

Motivating factor	Reality of the job (1–5)	Personal motivator (1–5)
Money		
Challenge		
Freedom		
Status		
Praise		
Thanks		
Responsibility		
Being in control		
Convivial working atmosphere		
Relaxed atmosphere		
Sense of order		
Competition		

What stresses you?

Again, if you identify the things that stress you most at work, you can consciously take action to minimise them. All jobs entail stress, and some entail a good deal, but you still want to reduce the stress as far as possible. I'm not talking here about positive pressure: many of us choose the jobs we do because we thoroughly enjoy working under stringent and challenging pressure, and are more stressed by boredom than by a tough deadline. Pressure becomes stress when it stops being fun and starts to generate negative emotions such as worry, frustration or anger.

Your boss cannot control every factor which stresses you, but they do have at least some power over many of them. Again, once you have identified these you can do something about them, for example:

- talk to your boss and explain the problem

- find your own ways to alleviate the stress

- find ways to deal with the stress, such as going for a run at lunchtime, talking it through with a friend, or even writing *I hate my boss* 20 times on a piece of paper (but don't ever let them find it).

Here's an exercise similar to the motivation one. Again, there's a list of stress factors, followed by two columns. In the middle one, mark on a scale of 1–5 how big a factor this is in your job. In the right-hand column score 1–5 according to how stressful you personally find this factor.

Motivating factor	Reality of the job (1–5)	Personal motivator (1–5)
Time pressure		
Difficult problems		
Difficult people (boss included)		
Poor communication		
Pressure from the boss		
Noise		
Lack of recognition		
Failure		
Working alone		
Negativity from boss and colleagues		

The danger signals, of course, are those factors which gain high scores in both columns. You'll find that simply analysing what stresses you is a big help in tackling it. You'll also find more detailed advice in Chapter 4 on certain types of boss-related stress, such as work overload, and having more than one boss.

ASSESSMENT TIME

Answer the following questions, but remember to keep the answers relevant to your boss. So you need to identify, for example, what your greatest strengths are in managing your particular boss:

- What are your two or three greatest strengths?
- What are your two or three greatest weaknesses?
- What motivates you most?
- What stresses you most?

CHAPTER 4

Work stress and how your boss can add to it

There are plenty of times for some people when stress is directly caused by a tricky boss. I hope this isn't the case for you but, if it is, there are plenty of other chapters in this book to help you. This chapter is about coping with the kind of stress that even the most amiable and co-operative boss sometimes generates – as do trickier bosses too. It's not personality stuff, it's simply the stresses that come with work.

However, that doesn't necessarily mean you have to put up with it. There are still ways of managing your boss when they create this kind of difficulty that will keep your stress levels down without disappointing your boss. The biggest areas of work stress that your boss contributes to are likely to be:

- interruptions
- work overload
- more than one boss

...so that's what we'll look at in this chapter.

Interruptions

Of course, interruptions are actually a big problem at busy times no matter who they come from. But interruptions from the boss are worse than most. They tend to assume that your time is theirs, so they have a right to interrupt you. And, while polite techniques are always the best with anyone, diplomacy is especially important with the boss.

It is infuriating if you're concentrating hard on something, in the middle of a train of thought, and your boss ambles in and starts talking about something that could easily have waited. Or perhaps they interrupt you just as havoc has broken out and you're frantically trying to meet a deadline that's just been pushed forward. How do you deal with it? Here are some techniques to use:

- At the risk of sounding obvious, one of the most effective is to say, as your boss appears in the doorway, 'I'm very busy on those figures you asked me for. Can this wait? I'll let you know as soon as I'm finished.' It won't always work, but it's the most honest and often the best way. After all, your boss has a vested interest in you doing the best job you can in the most effective way.

- Aim to visit your boss in their office rather than have them visit you. It's much easier to time the visit to suit you – even if it only gives you time to get to a good stopping point in the next couple of minutes – and you can keep the interruption much shorter. Once the boss has their feet under your desk it may be hard to shift them. Obviously you can't predict a lot of interruptions, but you can predict a fair proportion of them. Maybe you know your boss is planning to speak to you some time today about the agenda for next Monday's meeting. In that case, visit them before they visit you. Or perhaps they call you up and say, 'Got a few minutes? Good. I'll just pop down the corridor and see you.' In this case, reply, 'Don't bother, I'll come and see you. I have to go that way anyway.'

- If you have a task lined up which requires your undiverted concentration, try to schedule it when you know they'll be out of the office. If they tend to phone you when they're out, pick a time you know they'll be in a meeting. Even if they're in the building, you can still schedule these tasks for times when they're too busy to interrupt you.

Do-as-you-would-be-done-by

Treat your boss as you'd like them to treat you. It sends out a subliminal signal which won't cure a hardened interrupter on its own, but it will help to set an example. So don't interrupt your boss if you can help it – save several questions or points up for a single interruption; and always ask if this is a good time before launching into your interruption. At the very least, it gives you the moral high ground. You're not expecting anything of them that you don't already do yourself.

- If you know you need an uninterrupted spell, and you know your boss is likely to interrupt, clear it with them before you start. Say something like, 'I'd like to crack on with the report this afternoon, but I really need to be able to concentrate without interruptions. Is anything likely to crop up in the next few hours, or would this be a good time to do it?' Or you might ask them, 'Could I use the meeting room to work so that I can avoid interruptions?' Under cover of asking a question, you're actually making it clear you don't want to be disturbed. You could even ask, 'Is there anything you need me for before I get stuck into the report?'

- If you rarely shut the door to your office, simply doing so will send out a signal to everyone that you don't want to be disturbed. Often this works on the boss too.

- Divert your phone calls or switch on your voicemail to prevent your boss interrupting you by phone.

- If your boss is frequently inclined to visit and outstay their welcome, get rid of any extra chairs in your office. Or cover them with files. If

If you know you need an uninterrupted spell, and you know your boss is likely to interrupt, clear it with them before you start.

there's nowhere to sit and get comfortable, they'll leave much sooner.

- When your boss interrupts you, be as brief as you can with them without being rude. If you sit and chat to them for 10 minutes every time they interrupt, they can hardly be blamed for not realising you needed to get on with your work. So be brisk and businesslike without being brusque, and they'll soon get the point.

Everything in moderation

All these deterrent techniques work best if you use them in moderation. If your door is always shut and your phone always diverted, your boss (along with everyone else) will have little choice but to interrupt if they want to speak to you. But if they know that you only occasionally use these techniques when you genuinely need to, they are far more likely to respect them.

Work overload

The other interruption problem you can encounter with bosses, and a slightly trickier one, is when they interrupt you to give you additional work. A boss who likes to deposit more work on your desk without giving you time to complete the current load can be a major cause of stress.

Suppose you're busy working on a major proposal you have to have finished by Friday afternoon. It's a tight deadline as it is, given that you still have to keep on top of the routine work, phone calls and so on as well. Unexpectedly, your boss arrives and tells you that they want you to spend most of tomorrow attending a meeting on their behalf; it's an hour's travel each way and the meeting is scheduled to last all afternoon. There's no way you can complete the proposal by Friday if you take tomorrow out.

So what do you do? Many of us tend simply to take on the extra work without complaining for fear of angering or disappointing the boss. In order to complete the proposal that means working on it until late at night for the rest of the week. Stressful? You bet.

Another option many people go for is to take on the extra load without putting up much of a fight, and then deliver the proposal late. When the boss complains, they respond by pointing out that they lost a day going to that meeting last Wednesday. The boss is irritated by this, since they had no intimation that this would delay delivering the proposal.

Just don't make a habit of it

If your boss almost never dumps last-minute work on you, and only does so in an emergency, it may well be better to accept it. If it means working late an average of, say, an evening every month or two, it's probably worth it to cement the relationship with your boss (assuming you don't have personal commitments that make it impossible). Make sure your boss knows that you're putting yourself out, or there'll be no brownie points in it for you. Don't try to make them feel guilty, just let them know: 'It'll mean working late for a couple of nights. Yes, OK, I can do that.'

What are you supposed to do? The answer is to point out the problem to your boss, and make them take responsibility for it. Start by saying, 'I can go to the meeting tomorrow, but it will mean the proposal won't be finished until Monday. Is that all right with you?'

With luck, your boss will agree to this. But a lot of bosses won't. They make unhelpful and unconstructive comments such as, 'No, I need the proposal by Friday. I'm sure you'll manage it.' Don't stand for this. You need to be assertive (more on this in Chapter 7). If it can't be done, make it clear: 'I'm scheduled to work on this proposal from now right through until Friday. If I take a day out, that will add another day to my schedule. I shan't be able to deliver until Monday.'

If you still meet with an unhelpful, 'See what you can do' or 'I have to have the proposal on Friday', stand your ground. And ask your boss how it can be done: 'Can you suggest how I can complete the proposal by Friday if I'm not here tomorrow?' If your boss is inclined to do this to you frequently, you have to be assertive and stick to your guns. If it can't be done, keep telling them so politely but firmly until they get the message.

Don't settle for 'See what you can do' either. It means the boss hasn't accepted what you're saying, and will feel free to berate you when they don't get the proposal on Friday. They've never actually said it's OK to deliver a day later. The best response to 'See what you can do' is, 'I already know what I can do. I can only go to tomorrow's meeting if I deliver the proposal on Monday.'

Some bosses are very unorganised and frequently dump work on you at the last minute, simply because they forgot to give it to you in good time. This is very selfish behaviour, obviously, but more to the point it is extremely stressful working for this kind of boss. You simply have to be firm with them for your own sanity. If the technique outlined here doesn't stop them trying it on, use the feedback technique explained in Chapter 9.

Some bosses are very unorganised and frequently dump work on you at the last minute.

More than one boss

Here's a scenario that will make your heart sink if ever you've experienced it. If you have to deal with it now, chances are you find it a major source of stress, at least sometimes and quite possibly almost all the time – two bosses (more if fate really has it in for you), each of whom expects you to be available exclusively for them whenever they need you to be.

Play fair

Don't be tempted to play your bosses off against each other, or to mislead them about each other's workload. Sooner or later they will realise what you are doing, and will come to regard you as manipulative; they will stop trusting you. This not only damages your relationship seriously, but you'll also find that they don't believe you when you tell them for real that their demands are impossible to meet. And you'll have only yourself to blame.

Get them talking

The first step to handling multiple bosses is to get them talking to each other. Explain that you don't want to let either (or any) of them down, and that the best way to achieve this is for them to agree between them what your priorities should be. So if you know that one of them has a big project coming up, or another is going to be short-staffed until they fill that vacancy, anticipate trouble and ask them to meet with the other(s) in advance to discuss how much of your time should be allocated to each of them. Ideally, arrange to be at the meeting too if you can.

Anticipate trouble

The next stage is to anticipate shorter-term trouble yourself. If one of your bosses gives you a time-consuming task to do, ask them straight away to clear it with the others, or do so yourself. As soon as you can see your time is about to be filled without gaps for the next few days, make sure everyone is aware of the situation. That way, when you tell the second boss that your schedule has just been filled, they can say, for example, 'Ah. I'm going to need you to chase up those missing orders for me tomorrow morning. I'll talk to Janet now and see if she can spare you for half a day.'

This also has the advantage of keeping your bosses regularly reminded that they are not the only person you work for. Even on those occasions when they don't have a problem with your workload being filled by another boss, they'll still be reminded that they can't ever take your availability for granted.

Last-minute hiccups

Keeping your bosses in touch with each other and anticipating trouble will make a big difference. But there will still be times when one of your bosses tries to insist that you carry out a task that you simply don't have time for. Suppose they demand that you chase up the missing orders today, but that would mean you wouldn't get your other boss's research done by the time you agreed.

The answer here is to insist that they sort it out among themselves. Again, you need to use all your assertiveness skills (which you'll have acquired by the end of Chapter 7) to make sure that:

- they do not expect you to take responsibility for deciding whose work gets finished late
- they don't blame you for the situation they've got themselves into
- they don't use you as a go-between.

As a default setting, explain that you have to operate on a 'first come, first served' basis. The work you've already agreed to takes priority. You're happy to change this if everyone agrees to the change, but you need this boss to go away, clear any changes to your priorities with your other boss, and then let you know. Until you're told that *they* have collectively agreed a change, you'll carry on as planned.

Get confirmation

Unless you trust your bosses absolutely, make sure that the other boss really has agreed to change your priorities. The last thing you want is Janet saying, 'I've spoken to Paul, and he says he can wait until Thursday for you to chase the orders' only to have Paul demand to know why it hasn't been done on Wednesday. When you tell him what Janet said he insists he said no such thing, and blames you for changing your priorities without consulting him. So unless you trust her absolutely, tell Janet to get Paul to let you know – he can phone or email you if he's out of the office – that it's OK to give priority to her work.

As with the boss who tries to give you too much work, you have to be firm here. It is not your responsibility to make their decisions for them about priorities. So if they tell you that their work is desperately urgent and they can't get hold of your other boss, that's their problem. Be polite but firm: 'I'm sorry, but I can't let Paul down. If you can't contact him then I'm afraid I'll have to do his work first as I agreed with him.' Keep repeating it until they get the message. And you can point out that you'd do the same for them if the situation were reversed. Make sure that you would, too – don't ever show favouritism in your professional relationships with your bosses.

You may be wondering – what happens when one of your bosses is senior enough to overrule the other.

You may be wondering – and you will be if this applies to you – what happens when one of your bosses is senior enough to overrule the other. When Janet says, 'I don't care what Paul says – I'm overruling him. Get this urgent research done first and then chase his orders when you've finished this,' what do you do?

The answer is still the same: it's not your responsibility to sort out *their* problems. If Janet is authorised to overrule Paul, you'd better do as she tells you. Then get in touch with Paul and tell him the situation. Be firm if necessary and make it clear that if he's not happy you may sympathise but there's nothing you can do. If he wants to sort it out, he'll have to talk to Janet. If he asks you to talk to her, refuse politely: 'No, the only way to sort it out is for you to talk to her directly. I'll just end up as a go-between and nothing will get resolved. If you want her to change her mind, you'll have to talk to her.'

If you are consistently assertive with your bosses when problems crop up, and you refuse to get drawn into making decisions for them or acting as a go-between, they'll soon learn to stop asking you to take on responsibility for prioritising between them. They will have to be united in the instructions, and the changes, that they give you. And your stress levels will drop wonderfully – and deservedly – as a result.

CHAPTER 5

Create the perfect relationship with your boss

We've tackled the business of eliminating the negative aspects of your relationship with your boss. That goes a long way towards managing them well. But you can do more, and you'll need to for a really top relationship with them. That's what this chapter is all about: the extra distance you can go to capitalise on the good work you've done so far, and create a relationship your colleagues will envy and your boss will treasure.

You'll find here the top 10 dos and top 10 don'ts for creating a truly terrific working relationship with your boss. These are all tips which will earn you extra brownie points. They're not about crawling or sucking up to the boss – simply working in a way which will make their life easier and more pleasant. And it will all be down to you.

Do...

1 ...be popular

This doesn't mean you have to be a creep, nor even that you should never be tough – sometimes that's necessary. The point is that you should always be polite and courteous to everyone you encounter, and show appreciation when others are helpful to you; if you do this you are bound to be popular and well liked.

Your boss will notice the way you treat other people, and will be far more impressed if you are always pleasant to everyone than if you are rude or offhand with people who are below you on the ladder. You need to be courteous with colleagues, customers and other contacts. Your boss's life will be a whole lot easier if other people are happy to deal with you and do business with you.

Being popular to do business with is not only a matter of being civil to the people you deal with. It also means giving them good service. So whoever you're dealing with, customers or junior colleagues from other departments, follow a code of practice:

- Always reply to messages promptly.
- Always return phone calls when you say you will.
- Always meet any commitments you make (so don't make any you won't be able to meet).

These simple practices are very important because they send a message to the person concerned that you take them seriously. If you don't reply to someone's messages, call them when you say you will, or fulfil your commitments to them, you are in effect telling them they're not worth the bother. Earn yourself a reputation for being popular, considerate and polite, and your boss will feel confident in asking you to deal with other people.

2 ...be willing to do a little extra

Any boss is grateful to have someone on the team who is happy to put themselves out from time to time. Even if home commitments mean you can never work overtime, it doesn't mean you can't show willing in other ways during normal hours.

Suppose there's a bug going round and you're short-staffed. Someone is needed to provide emergency cover on the sales desk for the morning, or to sit on reception over lunch. If you volunteer, it shows the boss you're enthusiastic about the job and that you want to make other people's lives a little easier (including theirs).

There are plenty of opportunities to give a little more than your job description commits you to, from helping out another department to agreeing to write an article for the next issue of the company news-letter. Apart from the helpfulness of actually doing the task, being a willing volunteer also saves your boss the time and stress of having to nag the team into helping.

3 ...identify with the organisation

If you're a true corporate player, you will be rooting for the organisation and enjoy its successes. When things are going well in the company, the division or the department, you'll be cheering along as part of the team. Your boss will be pleased to see that you feel involved and loyal to the organisation.

The alternative is to regard the organisation as a separate entity, as many people do. They refer to the company as 'them' rather than 'us', and treat its successes as though they had happened to an organisation unconnected with them. If you do this you effectively indicate to your boss that you don't feel any loyalty to the organisation, and that you don't care about it. Since your job is ultimately to bring the greatest possible benefit to the organisation, it's hard to see quite how you'll be motivated to do this when you feel no attachment to it.

So make sure your boss can see that you are part of the family, and that you recognise that what is good for the organisation is good for you too.

Us and them

Some organisations have an 'us' and 'them' culture, in which most employees regard senior management as being apart from them, and sometimes speak of them disparagingly or even contemptuously. As a general rule, it is the fault of senior management if this kind of culture is allowed to thrive. Nevertheless, if you work in this kind of company you can still make yourself the exception rather than the rule. It will make your boss's job easier, and will give the impression that you really belong.

4 ...take criticism well

Any reasonable boss will criticise you only when they believe it's justi-fied. More often than not, they're probably right. Many people react very defensively to being criticised and try to justify their actions. Some even get angry or upset. These reactions make it hard for the boss to encourage someone to grow and learn from their mistakes, and make them dread having to give criticism to such people – even though they know it's their job to do so.

How much more pleasant the boss's job would be if their constructive criticism were met by a mature and relaxed response. If you can provide this, you'll make yourself very popular. What you need to do is:

- admit any mistakes or shortcomings. Not only is this a sign of strength, but it also reassures the boss that you are fully aware of where you've gone wrong

- show your boss appreciation for bringing your mistake to your atten-tion. You can say something like, 'Thanks for pointing that out to me. I've learnt something useful, and I'll be able to do better next time'.

Your boss will be relieved and impressed by your maturity and your strength of character in being able to handle criticism so well.

5 ...write competently

We can't all write brilliantly, but we should all be able to write compe-tently. A poor writing style will show up every time you write an email or memo, let alone a report or proposal or a longer document. To those who cannot write or spell this may be acceptable, but if your boss and other superiors can write competently, they will be disappointed in you. They will be wary of showing anything you've written to other people because it will reflect badly on the department and the organisation.

So if your writing isn't up to scratch, you need to brush up on it. Learn how to write better by going to evening classes, reading books on how to write, or getting a friend or colleague to coach you. In the meantime, here are a few pointers to improving your writing style:

- Don't try to impress your readers with long words and jargon, or cleverly constructed sentences. You will only come across as pompous, and you're more likely to make mistakes. Aim for simple but clear writing, and short sentences. Not only does this read better, it's also far easier to do if writing isn't your strong point.

- Good layout is important as well as spelling, grammar and punctuation. You will give an instant good impression if any document, from a letter to a report, is well laid out and looks professional. Don't cram each page full of text, but leave comfortable margins and space around headings.

- For longer documents, use plenty of subheadings, bullet pointed lists and short paragraphs (they should be wider on the page than they are deep) to make the material look interesting and approachable.

- If you've written an important document, get someone whose writing, spelling and grammar are good to check it through for you.

- Don't rely on computer spellcheckers. They're great for a first sweep through a piece of writing, but they miss a great deal of mistakes. They will tell you only if you write something that isn't a word. But many spelling mistakes result in genuine words that simply aren't the right ones. For example, if you miss the final 'f' from 'off' the computer will see a real word, 'of', and not correct it. So by all means

Don't rely on computer spellcheckers. They're great for a first sweep through a piece of writing, but they miss a great deal of mistakes.

use a spellchecker for an initial round of corrections, but check through the piece yourself, or get someone else to do it.

Moving up the ladder

Many people get key promotions as a result of reports they've written, partly because reports – good ones at least – tend to be circulated around the higher echelons of the organisation so they get you noticed. This is one reason why your writing style is so important. You wouldn't want to produce a report with brilliant content but which failed to impress as it should because it was so poorly written.

---

6 ...be open-minded

Organisations can grow only by changing. Paradoxically, change is a constant feature of most successful companies. So the job of management – including that of your boss – means spending a lot of time driving through change. One of the most frustrating things for bosses is finding that their team members resist the kind of changes they need to promote. Team members who are open to change and happy to embrace it are therefore highly popular with their bosses. What's more, if you can welcome change, it marks you out as being management material compared with those who instinctively resist it.

Being open to change doesn't simply mean agreeing to go along with it, although that's a good start. If you really want to be seen as an open-minded member of the team, you can actively promote change, suggest new ideas and help to find ways to make any necessary changes work well. That way, you're not simply cheering from the sidelines; you're in the thick of the change game.

7 ...accompany every problem with a solution

Some people just complain, complain, complain. They can't deliver this order on time because there's always a bottleneck in despatch. They don't see how this idea can work because it'll cost too much. They don't want to invite this client for a meeting because there's nowhere suitable in the building to meet.

If you're seen as this kind of persistent complainer, you'll frustrate your boss and gain a reputation for being negative and unconstructive. In a way it can seem unfair: maybe there *is* always a bottleneck in despatch. Or the idea on the table *is* too costly. Or there *isn't* a presentable meeting room. So what are you supposed to do? Keep quiet about it and let the problems continue?

Of course not. All you have to do is to come up with a solution. Not a sarcastic, obviously flawed one ('I'll just get on the plane to Bahrain and deliver it myself, shall I, since despatch can't seem to get it there?'). You need to find a solution that is better than the present option, even if it isn't perfect. For example:

- Post the urgent package first-class yourself, and then offer to work with despatch to propose a solution to their bottleneck problems.

- Suggest ways in which the costly idea could be modified to bring the costs down, or ways in which the money could be found to finance it.

- Explain the problem with not having somewhere suitable to see your client, and ask to take them out for a lunch meeting. Then recommend a feasible way to turn one of the offices into an occasional meeting room that could be smart and presentable.

By doing this you are drawing your boss's attention to exactly the same problem, but you're doing it in a way that makes you look like a fixer, a problem-solver, a solutions-person. In other words, just the kind of person your boss wants at their right hand. So the rule is simple: every time you bring a problem or complaint to your boss's attention, couple it with a workable solution.

Add to the fun

If you get into the habit of looking for solutions rather than presenting problems to others and expecting them to solve them, you'll soon find that your whole outlook on work becomes more positive, and you start to see difficulties as challenges rather than problems. You may well find this change of emphasis means that you enjoy work far more, and find it more motivating than before.

---

8 ...praise but don't flatter

What's the difference between praise and flattery? If you are sincere, genuine and measured in your remarks, you are praising. If you are insincere or excessive in your praise, it becomes empty flattery.

Your boss needs praise just as much as you do. Perhaps they get it from their boss, perhaps they don't; either way their boss isn't in such close proximity to them as you are, so they're bound to miss out on a lot of praise for what they do. However, you can fill in the gaps, by making sure that you give your boss praise when it's due.

You want to be certain that you come across as being genuine and not a creep. Apart from anything else, once your praise turns to empty flattery (or appears to), it ceases to be worth anything to your boss. To make sure this doesn't happen:

- praise your boss only when you genuinely mean it

- don't go over the top. A simple, 'I liked the way you handled that' or 'Hmm. Impressed!' is often sufficient

- save the really strong praise for those big successes that come only occasionally – clinching a major contract or solving a serious problem

- don't just focus on the boss if their achievement is shared with anyone else – distribute your praise to everyone involved.

9 ...be loyal

We've already touched on loyalty to the organisation, which is certainly important. But of course you also need to show loyalty to your boss personally, not only in their presence but also when they're not there – in front of the team, other colleagues, senior management, customers and suppliers. In other words, loyalty is a permanent thing. You can't pick it up sometimes and drop it at others.

On a personal level, loyalty to the boss means no gossiping about them behind their back, on personal or professional topics. Sometimes there may be a genuine need to discuss the boss with your immediate colleagues, but make sure you say nothing that is unfair, unjustified or irrelevant to the discussion. In particular, never give away any confidence about the boss no matter what. And your boss shouldn't have to tell you that something is confidential. Suppose they confided in you once that their marriage was shaky; this kind of information should automatically be treated as confidential. Even if a colleague tells you that the boss told them too, that still doesn't entitle you to divulge any details which may have been given to you alone.

Loyalty to your boss means not only resisting gossip and criticism, but also actively backing them up. Some bosses don't make this easy for you; nevertheless, if one of your boss's fellow managers criticises the boss in front of you, you need to stand up for them. Remember, the other manager may disagree with you, but privately they'll be thinking, 'I hope my team members would stick up for me like that.'

Another aspect of loyalty is backing the boss up in front of them when they're being attacked by others. Obviously in the line of amicable discussion of, say, a new idea, you should feel free to express your personal opinion (unless your boss asks you to do otherwise). But if things turn unpleasant or personal, or other people are criticising your boss's past actions, you need to give them all your support. If you privately share some of the other people's views you can say so privately to your boss later if you wish. But in public, showing loyalty is more important than voicing your personal opinion.

Careless talk

As a rule of thumb, before you say anything about your boss ask yourself how you would feel if it got back to them. If you're making a genuine, relevant and fair criticism in front of friends, you should be able to justify it easily to the boss if ever you had to. But if you feel uncomfortable at the thought of having to justify remarks made out of place – either unfair comments, or fair but made to the wrong people – then bite your tongue.

---

10 ...under-promise and over-deliver

This is a great rule for dealing with everyone, and especially bosses. Not only does it prevent you disappointing people by letting them down, it goes further and gives you the chance actively to impress the boss and anyone else you apply it with.

The principle is very simple. You promise less than you feel you should be able to manage. So if your boss asks you to complete a task by Friday and you reckon you can do it by Wednesday, you keep quiet about your own assessment and you simply agree to Friday. Then, when all goes to plan, you're done by Wednesday and you deliver more than you prom-

Never give the earliest time you think you can manage – you can only disappoint if things go wrong and you're late.

ised – the task's done *and* it's two days early. What's more, if your world happens to collapse around your ears earlier in the week, you've built in two days' leeway and you should still complete the task on time – by Friday.

This approach can't fail to impress. Often you'll be asked to say when you complete a task. Never give the earliest time you think you can manage – you can only disappoint if things go wrong and you're late. Always give the latest you feel is acceptable and that your boss will agree to. Then your *worst* scenario is that you still meet the deadline. Very often we're talking about shorter timescales. Tell the boss you can get something done in an hour when you know it should take only half an hour. Tell them you'll get back to them with figures after lunch when you hope you should have them ready by mid-morning. You're just constantly setting yourself up to impress.

This works with things other than deadlines; it also applies to standards. For example, you might tell the boss you can get the figures for this year by the end of the day, but you won't have the past three years' figures until tomorrow. Privately you reckon you should have them all by 5 o'clock, but you're building in some leeway, and the boss will be delighted if your private view is right and you've got the whole lot by close of play today.

Or you might tell your boss that when you negotiate the upcoming deal with one of your suppliers, you reckon you can get the discount you're after, but that quality guarantees may not improve. Privately, you're hoping to get an increase in quality guarantees too.

Don't...

1 ...splash out on expenses

Nobody expects you to forego your business expenses, but the way that you use your expense account says a lot about you. If you spend the most you can get away with, always taking customers out for expensive meals, or staying at the best hotels, the implication is that:

- you are extravagant and don't know the value of money

- you can barely be trusted with a budget

- you're happy to fleece the company

- you don't care about your boss's budget constraints.

None of these says a lot for you as an employee. If, on the other hand, you're sensible with your expenses and can easily justify everything you spend, you'll look reliable, trustworthy and loyal. So don't book into the grottiest hotel, or take your customers for lunch at the local greasy spoon café, but show moderation and your boss will notice and appreciate it.

Risking your reputation

The closer you come to overspending your expense account, the greater danger there is that your boss will start to question why you're spending so much. There's an increasing danger they will suspect that you may be fiddling some claims. Even if they can't prove it (very possibly because you're not doing it) they will be left with lingering doubts about your honesty.

---

2 ...badmouth your ex-boss

When you speak critically of an ex-boss, what do you suppose your present boss thinks? Do you imagine they feel sorry for you working for such a difficult manager, and resolve to make your life more pleasant in future? No, they don't. Here's what they actually think:

- 'There are two sides to every story. I wonder what really happened?'
- 'Is this what they'll be saying about me once I become their ex-boss?'
- 'What a negative attitude. If they haven't got anything good to say, they shouldn't say anything at all.'

The fact is that all your comments about your ex-boss may be entirely justified – understated even – but that's not the impression you'll give to your present boss. Every impression you give to them is a poor one, so don't badmouth the ex-boss, whether they're from your present organisation or a different one.

The same goes for your former company. Badmouthing the last organisation you worked for (or any others) shows disloyalty and makes your boss wonder what you'll be saying about your present company in a few years' time.

3 ...complain about menial tasks

From time to time, we all need to do tasks outside our normal routine which some might consider beneath them. Whether the boss asks you to fetch extra chairs, cover on reception at lunchtime or stuff envelopes, you need to show that you're happy to perform these tasks.

Your boss wouldn't be asking you to do these things unless there were a good reason. Maybe there's some kind of crisis underway, or perhaps you're seriously short-staffed. If you say no to doing them, you give the impression of being arrogant and full of your own importance. More importantly, however, you also show that you've missed the point.

Your boss is looking at the bigger picture: the immediate priority is simply to get the chairs moved before the customers arrive. Who actually does the job is secondary. If you won't co-operate, you're demonstrating that you aren't capable of seeing where the team's priorities lie, but can see only your own narrow role. If, however, you muck in cheerfully, you show the boss that you are a real team player who, like them, has an eye on the bigger issue.

4 ...bear grudges

You cannot work effectively as part of a team if you sulk when you're put out, or if you bear grudges. Your boss will quickly become frustrated with anyone who upsets the team's balance and morale by creating an atmosphere or allowing disagreements to fester.

If you are unhappy with your boss, a team mate or any close working colleague, either address the problem head-on (you can use the feedback techniques in Chapter 9) or forget about it. But whatever you do, don't bear a grudge.

5 ...go over your boss's head

One surefire way to irritate your boss is to go direct to their boss without consulting them first. It's disrespectful and it undermines their authority. It also implies that you don't think they know their job, and you're telling their boss that too. Altogether not surprising, then, if it damages your relationship with them.

Clearly this rule applies to complaining about your work or even about your boss. But it also applies to putting forward ideas. If you have an important proposal to put forward, take it to your boss before you show it to any other managers, and let *them* be the one to take it forward.

6 ...confront the boss in front of other people

Never wash your dirty linen in public. If you're unhappy with your boss, save it until the two of you can discuss it in private. Your boss will never forgive you if you embarrass or humiliate them in front of other people, and you'll look pretty shoddy yourself to the people who witness your outburst.

Diplomacy first

If you feel strongly that you have no option but to go direct to your boss's boss, think hard about alternative approaches. One compromise solution can be to go to several managers simultaneously including your boss. For example, you might copy other managers in on an email to your boss if you're warning of the dangers of a decision which you believe will be catastrophic for the organisation and you can't convince the boss without their support. Even so, you should avoid this approach unless you have exhausted all other possibilities.

It doesn't matter how justified you are in your complaint, you are never justified in making it public. Bite your tongue if necessary and don't let your anger or frustration out until the appropriate time – which won't be until you've calmed down anyway. Use the guidelines in Chapters 9 and 10 to help you deal with conflict with your boss, and keep it behind closed doors.

7 ...repeat mistakes

It's natural to make mistakes, and your boss knows that. Great scientists such as Thomas Edison, Linus Pauling and Albert Einstein explained that you couldn't achieve successes without notching up failures on the way. And if making mistakes was good enough for Einstein, it's good enough for us.

What the likes of Edison and Einstein did, however, was to make sure they never made the same mistake twice. That is a waste of time and teaches you nothing. Each time you make a mistake you need to learn from it so that you are closer to the next success.

Your boss expects you to make mistakes, but also expects you to learn from them. They want to know that once you've got something wrong, they can count on you never to get it wrong again. So make sure you don't repeat your mistakes, and reassure your boss by being clear that you know where you've gone wrong and can prevent it recurring. For example, 'I can see now that if I'd phoned to confirm the booking I'd have found out in time that there was a problem, so I need to do that in future. Whenever I make a booking I'll put a note in my diary for nearer the time to phone and confirm it. That way, this can't happen again.'

8 ...gossip

We've already established that you shouldn't bitch about your boss or your ex-boss. But you don't want to get yourself a name as a gossip generally. Gossip is far more common and damaging in organisations where communications are poor than in those which communicate well. But even in well-run companies, gossip about the organisation is the bane of management's life.

Rumours can fly round an organisation – closures, lay-offs, big changes for better or worse – and can do a huge amount of damage to management/staff relations. Don't be a part of this, or you'll be branded a troublemaker.

Gossip about other people in the organisation is far less damaging to management as a rule (unless it's about them), but your boss is unlikely to draw the same distinction you do between different types of gossip. If you're labelled a gossip, you're labelled a gossip and that's that. And your boss will think that you rumour-monger or bitch about them even if you don't. The only safe course is to steer well clear of the gossips around the coffee machine, and be seen to be above all that.

Gossip is far more common and damaging in organisations where communications are poor than in those which communicate well.

Ask for clarification

If there's a rumour going round about critical decisions or changes to the organisation, your best bet is to go to the boss yourself. Don't mention names or get the gossips into trouble. Just explain that you thought management should know what is being said, and should be warned that if they don't communicate the correct facts to their employees, the gossip is likely to get worse. Doing this sets you apart from the gossips (despite the fact that you've obviously been listening to them), and supports management without getting any of your colleagues into trouble.

9 ...bother your boss when they're busy

Your boss doesn't have only you to bother them when they're busy. They have a whole team of people to pester them at inconvenient moments. Wouldn't it be nice to be the one your boss could count on to leave them alone just when it's most critical?

Learn to recognise when your boss is busy or preoccupied, and don't disturb them. If they're completing a project to a tight deadline, or rushing to a meeting they're on the verge of being late for, give them a break. Here are some ways to make your interruptions as few and as convenient as possible:

- Anticipate problems so you have time to wait for a good moment to discuss them with the boss.

- Collect together several minor questions or discussion points and then disturb your boss just once to deal with all of them.

- If you phone your boss or stick your head round the door, always start by asking 'Have you got five minutes?' or 'Is this a good moment?'

- For anything that requires privacy or needs some time to discuss, make an appointment with the boss. However, don't irritate by asking for a meeting every other day – save it for the issues which really warrant it.

- Be aware of the pressures your boss is under so you can avoid disturbing them at times when they are very pressured.

If you follow all these guidelines, you'll almost never have to bother your boss at a difficult time. And when you do interrupt them, which will be in only genuine emergencies, your boss will know that you must have a valid reason to do so – unlike most of the rest of the team who pester them without consideration.

10 ...upstage your boss

Your boss may be a shy retiring type or an egocentric megalomaniac. Either way, they like to be praised and given the limelight from time to time, even if they don't give that impression. So make sure that when they are praised by other people you don't get in the way.

This isn't the time to point out your contribution to the success in question, nor to mention how much luck the project needed to succeed. This is the time to help direct the focus on to your boss and their achievement. If they are magnanimous enough to mention that they couldn't have done it without the support of the team, that's great. If they aren't that generous...well, that's their prerogative. Comfort yourself with the fact that their success is bound to reflect well on the rest of you without their help.

PART II

Building your skills

As well as understanding your boss and learning to work more effectively with them, you also need to build up a raft of skills for dealing with people generally. They will all be important when managing your boss; they will also be useful for managing your relationships with colleagues and subordinates. And what's more, you'll still need them when you or your boss move on and you find yourself working with a new manager who may be very different.

CHAPTER 6

How to cope with emotions

There are times when getting on with the boss is a doddle. Everything's going well, you know what you're doing and you can do it well. And then there are the other times. When you're under stress – or the boss is – there's a tendency to get emotional. You may be winding each other up, or outside factors may be making one or both of you stressed. Either way, you can end up taking it out on each other if you're not careful.

Heightened emotions, unless they are positive ones, get in the way of a good working relationship. So you need to be able to control your own emotions, and you also need to be able to handle your boss's emotions so that you can calm them down rather than inflame them. These techniques, of course, apply to handling emotions in anyone else, not only the boss.

Your emotions

The first step to handling unconstructive emotion in other people is to stay calm, so it stands to reason that the first skill to master is controlling your own emotions. With many bosses this is rarely a problem, but with some it can certainly be a challenge. Whether they make you feel angry, irritable, tearful or anything else, you need to find a way to keep on top of your response.

I'm not suggesting that your response may not be entirely justified. But showing your emotions is never going to be the quickest or the most effective way to resolve things in the short term, nor the best step towards a good relationship in the long term. What's more, to the kind of boss who provokes this response, your display of feeling can come across as emotional blackmail. It may appear to say, 'Look what you've done! You made me cry/get angry/get irritable...' As soon as emotional blackmail – real or imagined – enters the equation, you're in trouble. That starts to look like game-playing and manipulation, and you don't want to be a part of that since it makes a strong relationship with your boss impossible. A good relationship must be based on honesty and trust.

All this doesn't mean you should bottle up your emotions. As you'll see later, especially in Chapters 8 and 10, you should certainly express how you feel. But you need to express it calmly in words, not by emotional demonstration. And to do that, you have to be able to stay calm. Once you're calm, you can choose your words carefully to make sure that what you say is constructive rather than confrontational.

Separate home and work

Although you should aim to present as calm a front as you can at work, and not be given to bouts of rage, sulking or tears, there is an exception. You are allowed to be tearful about non-work related upsets. This should happen rarely if ever, but if you've just taken a phone call telling you about a family bereavement, for example, you're not expected to bite your tongue and show no response. You're allowed to be human.

Some of us find staying calm easier than others. If you find it tough, here are a few ideas to help you:

- Focus on your objective, which is to resolve the conflict that is generating these feelings. Recognise that staying calm will help you achieve this faster and more effectively.

- Use the approaches in Chapters 8 and 10 to resolve things without emotional displays.

- If someone's behaviour makes you feel tearful or angry, don't listen to it. Once you've got the point, they are probably repeating themselves anyway if they're angry. So look them in the eye and count to twenty, or think about something that makes you happy. In any case, you're not going to be able to resolve things until they're also calm and reasonable.

- If they are emotional, use the techniques later in this chapter to calm them down.

- If you feel unable to restrain your emotions, just leave. If you need to give a reason, be honest: 'I'm feeling too emotional to discuss this now. I'm going to leave, and I'll discuss it with you when I feel calmer.'

The boss's emotions

Once you've learnt to control your emotions, you can start to handle your boss's emotions, too, from a position of strength. Now you're calm and rational, you are in a far better position to get your boss back on track. Probably the most common emotion you're likely to encounter from your boss is anger, so we'll look at how to handle that first.

There are two types of anger you might encounter from your boss: justified anger and unjustified or tactical anger. You need to handle these two emotions in very different ways.

Justified anger

The best bosses don't make emotional displays of anger no matter how out of line you are. They express their feelings through words, not

Once you've learnt to control your emotions, you can start to handle your boss's emotions, too.

actions. But there are times when the boss is entitled to be angry with a team member (though I'm sure this would never happen to you).

Let the punishment fit the crime

For anger to be justified it must be in proportion to the offence. If your boss spends three hours screaming at you for being two minutes late for the first time in a year, that's not justified anger. But if they spend 10 minutes sounding off at you for a stupid mistake that has cost the organisation £20,000 in sales, that's justified (even if it would have been better to handle it without raising their voice).

So what do you do when your boss gives you a legitimate dressing down? If you're out of line, the answer is that you:

- admit it
- apologise
- offer to make reparation if it's possible.

It's as simple as that.

There is another category of justified anger, however, which you are far more likely to encounter (since you would never make stupid mistakes such as the example above). Your boss may be understandably angry about something which is actually a misunderstanding, or which you couldn't have foreseen the result of. Suppose they've just got into trouble with *their* boss because their budget is late – the reason being that you still haven't submitted the figures they need from you. No wonder they're angry. In fact, you've been badly let down by a supplier who kept promising you the figures you needed but never came up with them.

The result is that your boss calls you in and you can see they're very angry at being let down. How do you handle the situation and defuse the boss's anger? For a start, you stay calm as we've already seen. But then what?

- People who get angry for a legitimate reason tend to do so because they feel they won't get the response they want otherwise. They fear they won't be listened to or taken seriously. Your boss is worried that if they don't get angry with you, you won't learn for next time the importance of getting the figures in on time. So the first thing to do is to listen fully to them (follow the guidelines in Chapter 8) so they can see you're taking in what they're saying.

- Now show them you feel their anger is justified. Not necessarily that directing it at you is justified, but that anger is an understandable response. Legitimise their feelings by sympathising with them (without apologising if it's not your fault): 'I can see why you're feeling angry,' or 'You must be incredibly frustrated.'

- Don't spend ages justifying your actions. It will just sound as if you're making excuses. They're angry about their own problems: they don't want to hear a sob-story about yours. So you can say, 'There's a delay because I can't get Simpson's to give me their figures,' but then leave it at that. The truth here is that you should find a way to prevent such misunderstandings – in this instance you could have warned the boss that you were having problems getting the figures – so although the root problem may not be your fault, you're responsible at least for poor communication.

- In the end, people who are angry (your boss or anyone else) want a result. So once you've shown that you understand their anger, offer a solution. For example, tell them you'll go to another supplier for prices, or that you'll get on to Simpson's again and if there's no result in 48 hours you'll get back to the boss about it. If there's also a poor communication problem, acknowledge this and show that it won't happen again. So you might say, 'I'll get on to Simpson's again, and I'll try to get prices out of Sergeant's too, and Burke's. I'll have figures from at least one of them for you by Tuesday. And I can see now that I should have warned you that Simpson's were letting me down; another time I'll tell you in good time if I can't meet a deadline.'

If your boss's anger is justified you'll find that, once you've been through these steps, they will calm down because there's nothing left for them to be angry about. You've appreciated the seriousness of the problem, acknowledged their anger, agreed a solution and shown that it won't happen again.

> ### A promise is a promise
>
> If you've agreed a solution with your boss, you must stick to your side of it. If you encounter problems, say so before it's too late and get your boss's input into how to deal with them. Otherwise their anger will be even more justified next time.

Tactical anger

While some people's anger is genuine, others use anger as a weapon to intimidate you into giving in to them. This is a particularly difficult emotion to handle when it comes from your boss, who is already in a position of authority over you. Obviously this means they don't need to use such tactics to get you to carry out tasks it is your job to do; a simple instruction is enough. But what about using anger to intimidate you into, for instance:

While some people's anger is genuine, others use anger as a weapon to intimidate you into giving in to them.

- doing tasks you're not obliged to

- working longer hours than your contract stipulates

- backing ideas you don't agree with

- handling other people – perhaps your own subordinates – in ways you don't wish to

- misleading other people on their behalf, or even lying to cover for them.

People use anger tactically because they have found it works. Like throwing tantrums, they probably discovered as small children that they could get what they wanted this way, and they've kept on using the tactic ever since. The way to counter this is to let the boss see that this approach doesn't work on you. This means you'll have to be assertive (see the next chapter), and not give in to them when they treat you in this way. Eventually (I can't pretend it works overnight) they'll realise they're wasting their breath and they'll stop using this tactic with you.

The assertive approach to handling tactical anger means refusing to allow it in your presence:

- Say something like, 'I'm not prepared to be shouted at, and I shall leave if you don't calm down.'

- If they don't stop, carry out your threat: leave the room. You can say, 'I'll talk to you when you're calmer,' or simply say, 'Excuse me,' and go.

- If they repeat the outburst at the next encounter, repeat your response to it. Keep on doing this until they learn to deal with you calmly and rationally.

There's no denying that a lot of people find the prospect of talking to the boss in this way somewhat scary, to say the least. But once your boss starts behaving like this, you're actually dealing with a five-year-old, not a manager. They may be senior to you in the organisation, but on a personal level we're all equals, and you have the right to be treated respectfully.

There's nothing the boss can do to you for standing up to them; if they try other emotional games with you, you can simply respond assertively to those too. But it shouldn't come to that – if you've built an otherwise good relationship with your boss they will learn quickly not to use this tactic on you. They will respect you more for defending your rights calmly but firmly than they did when you used to buckle under the force of their anger.

Feedback techniques (see Chapter 9) also work well in convincing your boss to drop this unconstructive behaviour. One of the advantages of feedback is that it enables you to raise the issue at a time when the boss isn't angry, so it can be resolved calmly and reasonably. You could use feedback to let your boss know that in future you won't remain in the room if they start shouting at you.

Positive spiral

One of the many reasons for managing your boss well and building a strong working relationship is that it makes it far easier to deal with issues like tactical anger employed against you. Refusing to give in can give rise to all sorts of unpleasantness if you do it in the context of a tricky relationship. But when you've built a relationship that is otherwise sound, honest and trusting, your boss will respond positively when you decline to play their game.

Sulking

In many ways, sulking is an alternative to anger. Most children tend towards either tantrums or sulking; few regularly use both. Many of us opt for one or the other in our personal relationships, too, when our

People sulk because they want to let you know how upset they are.

emotions get the better of us. The same goes for those adults who are not mature enough to keep their displays of emotion away from their work.

People sulk because they want to let you know how upset they are. They feel that if they didn't sulk you would think the matter wasn't important to them. Almost all of us are prone to sulk occasionally, but some people do it over such seemingly minor issues that it ends up happening frequently and creates an unpleasant and unhelpful atmosphere that can seriously sour the working relationship. When your boss is a sulker, things can get very unpleasant, so here are a few tips for handling a situation:

- Silence is intended to make you feel guilty once you realise how upset or disappointed the boss is in you. Any approach to handling a sulking boss only works if you honestly have nothing to feel guilty about. So when you have the kind of discussion with your boss that can lead to an unpleasant silence, make sure you genuinely listen to them with an open mind, explain the reasons behind your view of the matter, and act in a friendly and reasonable way. Once the discussion is over, if they choose to sulk you know that there is nothing else you could have done except give in for no good reason, simply to avoid it.

- The aim is that you will capitulate. Never, ever do so. Just like using tactical anger, if it works for them once, they will try it every time.

- Don't make the atmosphere worse by being short with them either. If they give you the silent treatment, just say, 'OK, we'll sort it out later.' Then behave as if everything were normal, and as though they weren't sulking at all. Don't be tempted to try to cheer them up, or keep checking if they're OK. Sooner or later, they'll have to abandon the tactic when it becomes clear that it simply isn't working.

> **Check the facts**
>
> Remember that most of us sulk to some extent over major issues when we feel our feelings aren't being taken seriously. Even frequent sulkers occasionally have a genuine case – they really aren't being listened to or considered over something important. So always make a mental check when they get upset and satisfy yourself that this isn't one of those occasions – if it is, hear them out.

Tears

Unlike anger and sulking, it's unlikely that your boss is going to turn on the taps in order to get a response from you. Your subordinates sometimes do this if you're disciplining them or giving them bad news – when it's not genuine it's a form of emotional blackmail – but your boss will have little call to try this on you.

Nevertheless, with some bosses you may still encounter this emotion, and you need to know how to handle it. Some bosses are very sensitive, others are going through particularly major emotional upheavals. Whether your boss has just been bawled out by the MD, or whether they are going through a particularly horrendous divorce, what do you do if they burst into tears in front of you? Here are a few guidelines:

- Drop the boss/subordinate relationship for the duration, and treat them as you would any fellow human being who is upset.
- If you think they might prefer you not to be there, ask them, 'Would you prefer me to leave?' If you don't get a direct answer, stay with them unless the signals to go are strong.
- Let them talk, and you do the listening.

- Don't give them any advice unless they specifically ask for it, and preferably not then either.

- Next time you see the boss you can ask, 'How are you feeling?' but don't make a big thing of it, or ask them repeatedly, unless they encourage it. They may well be embarrassed later, and be uncomfortable with any reference to the incident.

- No matter what they say or do, don't mention the episode to anyone else in or connected with the organisation. Your boss will appreciate and respect your ability to maintain their confidence, and it will build their trust in you. Betraying their confidence will do serious damage to your relationship.

- Unless your boss is also a close friend, don't mention the incident to them again unless they bring it up first. Most particularly, don't use it as any kind of emotional leverage, in other words don't remind them how sympathetic you were just as you're asking for a day off, or imply that they owe you a favour.

Positive emotions

Negative emotions such as anger, sulking and tears call for an assertive and calm response. But don't forget that you also need to respond appropriately to positive emotions. If your boss is delighted at this month's results, excited about tomorrow's presentation or thrilled about some personal success that they want to share with you, they will want to see a suitable response too.

If you want to build and maintain a strong relationship with the boss, you need to give them the reaction they are after when their emotions are positive. From their point of view, it's fairly demoralising if they proclaim enthusiastically that this month's figures are the best ever, only to have their announcement met with a shrug or a dismissive 'Really?'

So make sure that when your boss is enthusiastic and positive, you show empathy by responding positively to their emotion. Let them see that you understand how they feel – you feel the same too. It shows solidarity, and reassures them that you are a fellow spirit. And it makes your boss feel that you're the sort of person they like to have around.

7

How to be assertive

Assertiveness is a skill which very few of us are born with. We have to learn how to do it and, while many of us can do it some of the time, few of us can do it all the time without practice. So what is it? Before answering that question, let's just see if you recognise either of these scenarios.

Scenario 1

Your boss calls you in, looking very displeased. They've just been told by one of their fellow managers that you turned up half an hour late for a vital interdepartmental meeting yesterday. They are extremely disappointed – you've let the whole team down. You start to explain but they tell you there's no excuse for such behaviour. You mumble an apology and get out as fast as you can.

Scenario 2

OK, so that's not you. Let's try this version. Your boss calls you in, looking very displeased. They've just been told by one of their fellow managers that you turned up half an hour late for a vital interdepartmental meeting yesterday. They are extremely disappointed – you've let the whole team down. When you hear this, you're furious – it wasn't your fault. The manager in question changed the time and the message never reached you. You lay into your boss, complaining about the other manager, and the fact that your boss thinks you would do such a thing without a valid reason. Then you storm out.

If you're wondering which of these is supposed to be the assertive version, the answer is neither of them (OK, so you probably guessed that). In fact, assertiveness is the form of behaviour that prevents either of these scenarios from happening. So before we look in detail at how to be assertive, let's look at the alternatives to assertiveness, and why we don't want to use them. Assertiveness is a balanced approach between two extremes. If assertiveness is the fulcrum in the centre of the see-saw, the two opposite extremes are submission and aggression.

Submission

The first scenario is classic submissive behaviour. Rather than risk confrontation, we succumb to the temptation to take the easy route. Don't answer back, don't stand up to the boss in case it puts their back up. Submissive behaviour always means taking what appears to be the easy route, so it includes:

- keeping your feelings hidden
- saying what you think the other person wants to hear
- apologising even when it's not your fault
- taking on more work rather than saying 'no'
- allowing people to take advantage of you.

Recognise any of these? Many of us are submissive at least some of the time, at least with certain people – and the boss is often one of them. In the short term it avoids unpleasantness and conflict. So what's wrong with it?

Our submissive behaviour may work for everybody around us, but it doesn't work so well for us. Here are just a few examples of the damage it can do:

- Bottling up feelings can lead to dissatisfaction, demotivation and general work stress.

- For some people, hiding their feelings lasts only so long. Then they explode out in a display of aggression, which has its own disadvantages (as we'll see in a moment).

- Suppressing your feelings can also lead to resentment and ill-feeling towards the boss and anyone else you are submissive towards.

- If you never disagree openly with people, many of your best ideas never get aired. As well as being extremely frustrating, this means you're not making the contribution you should.

- Keeping your head down also makes it very hard for you to take the kind of risks or promote the controversial ideas that can earn you respect, reward and promotion.

- Apologising when it's not your fault will give people the impression that you *are* to blame.

- You can end up overworked through being unable to say 'no', and through allowing others to take advantage of your excessively good nature.

That should give you some idea as to why submissive behaviour isn't a good thing. It can lead to stress, demotivation, resentment, overwork, professional frustration, missing out on promotion and pay rises...to name but a few of the points against it.

Aggression

So what about the other end of the scale? Some of us behave aggressively because we feel that it gets us what we want. Some of us even do it when the pressure valve finally blows after all that submissive behaviour. So what is it that we think will get us what we want?

- Telling people exactly what we think rather than bottling up feelings – even when it is hurtful or offensive.

- Pushing our own ideas forward, at the expense of others' ideas if necessary.

- Telling people where to get off if they try to take advantage of us.

- Intimidating other people by raising our voices or using offensive or threatening language.

It's quite true that aggressive behaviour can often get us what we want – in the short term. And some of us aren't really *very* aggressive, after all; we're just a bit aggressive occasionally. That's OK, isn't it?

Well no, not really. Even displaying only occasional aggressive behaviour means that others are permanently aware of the threat of aggression from us. Occasional moderate aggression may not be as bad as frequent strong aggression, but it's still a bad thing.

But what's so wrong with using a technique that can get us what we want? Here's an idea of the problems an aggressive manner can bring:

- People often won't tell us things because of the risk of an aggressive response. For example, our colleagues may not tell us how our working relationship with them could be improved; our boss might not let us know what was wrong with the report we submitted (so how will we be able to improve on it next time and earn more credit?).

- We will get an unpleasant reputation among our colleagues, subordinates, boss and other managers, which will do nothing for our prospects of being given interesting and stimulating tasks, especially if they involve co-operating with others. And it will do nothing for our chances of promotion either.

It's quite true that aggressive behaviour can often get us what we want – in the short term.

- If we're pushy about our own ideas, other people's resentment may tempt them to reject our ideas for personal reasons, regardless of their merit.

- If we are offensive or hurtful to others, they are more likely to be offensive or hurtful to us.

- Adopting an intimidating or unpleasant tone when dealing with others means we will far more frequently find ourselves in arguments and conflicts, which are not the most effective way of resolving differences, since everyone tends to dig their heels in.

There. We'll get a bad reputation, we won't be told things we need to hear, our ideas are less likely to be adopted, people will treat us unpleasantly, we'll end up in more arguments and conflicts, and we'll damage our chances of promotion. That's not an exhaustive list, but it should be enough to persuade you that aggression is no smarter a tactic in the long run than submissiveness. So that just leaves us with the mid-point where the two behaviours balance out: assertiveness.

Assertiveness

Assertive behaviour carries all the advantages of both these extremes, without the disadvantages. It is an easy route to take, and it gets us what we want. What's more, it works in the long term as well as the short term. Now you've learnt the basic techniques you can be assertive all of the time instead of just some of the time, and you'll start to appreciate the benefits:

- You'll be able to express how you feel, without confrontation, so there'll be no more bottled-up feelings, frustrations and the stress that goes with it.

- Others will be able to respond to your feelings in a calm and measured manner, so that you feel your voice is heard.

- Your boss and others will be able to express their views and feelings to you, so you can rely on being told the things you need to hear.

- You'll learn to put forward even controversial ideas without conflict, so you can air all your views and feel more involved. People will be happy to accept your ideas if they agree with them.

- This means you'll be able to take credit for your own ideas.

- You'll earn a reputation for being easy to work with, so people will want you on the team for interesting and prestigious projects.

- You will earn the respect of your boss, your colleagues and your team.

- People will treat you with the respect that you give them, making your working relationships pleasant.

- You won't ever again find yourself overworked simply through being unable to say 'no'.

That's a pretty persuasive list of reasons why it's worth learning to be more assertive. Whichever end of the scale you tend to veer towards – submission or aggression, or even a mix of the two – assertiveness has got to be a better way. And it's not difficult. The only thing that takes practice is learning to suppress your habitual response, whether it's submissive or aggressive, and replace it with the assertive approach. Before long, assertiveness will become the habit, and you won't even have to think about it any more.

So how do you do this assertiveness thing? Well, there are five key skills you have to master. You probably use all of these at times, and some of them may already be no problem to you. It's just a matter of incorporating them all into your mainstream approach, rather than keeping them as an occasional add-on:

1. Show respect for other people.

2. Express your feelings.

3. Be honest.

4. Learn to stand your ground.

5. Be able to say 'no'.

We'd better look at each of these in turn.

Show respect for others

Here's one for the naturally aggressive among us. It's an important factor whatever your natural inclinations, but people with aggressive tendencies usually find it the hardest to master.

A large part of the principle of assertiveness is about respect, but it has to work both ways. If we are going to expect respect and fair treatment from others – which we will if we are assertive – we must give as good as we want to get. So showing respect for others is all about demonstrating the behaviour we want to receive back. So we need to:

- allow other people to have opinions without shouting them down or criticising them unfairly

- listen carefully when others are speaking (that's what the next chapter is all about)

- choose friendly and constructive ways of making negative comments

- speak calmly and fairly when we disagree with someone, without raising our voices, or becoming offensive or personal

- give encouragement to other people, and praise them when they do well.

Well done!

Yes, you can even praise the boss when they do well. There's no need to sound patronising, and so long as it's honest it won't sound sycophantic. Even bosses like to know that the people around them are impressed by them. So why not say, 'I never thought you'd pull that one off so success-fully!' or 'How did you get them to agree to such generous terms?' You can also praise them indirectly by asking for tips and advice: 'Negotiating's obviously one of your strong points. I'd love to sit in on a negotiation with a customer some time and see how you do it.'

We'd like to be on the receiving end of these behaviours, so we should demonstrate them to other people. And being assertive means behaving like this with everyone, not just a select few people whom we deal with frequently, or whom we think are useful to us.

If you're inclined towards aggression, just think how this new, assertive you could transform your relationship with your boss. They will change their view of you, and come to see you as a mature, pleasant person whom everyone – including them – is happy to work with.

Express your feelings

This one's for both the submissive and the aggressive. Submissive people need to learn to say what they feel, while the aggressive need to learn *how* to say it in a more assertive manner. As an assertive person, you recognise your right to express your feelings and have them heard;

If your boss – or anyone else – makes you feel angry, hurt, offended, sidelined, humiliated or anything else, the assertive response is to tell them so.

you also recognise others' right to be told your feelings in a way that won't upset them.

If your boss – or anyone else – makes you feel angry, hurt, offended, sidelined, humiliated or anything else, the assertive response is to tell them so. After all, if you don't tell them, how will they know? You deserve to have your feelings considered, but the boss doesn't have the option of doing this if you don't tell them how you feel.

There are several ways to tell someone how you feel. You could start by saying, for example:

- You're making me angry by...
- I don't like you saying...because...
- I feel...when you...
- You're being offensive...

Only one of these options is assertive; that is to say it expresses how you feel without provoking a confrontational response. (I'll tell you which one in a moment.) Your boss may not even realise the effect they're having on you, so if you show respect you won't want to upset them by being aggressive. If they *are* aware of the response they generate in you, you still don't want a confrontation. Apart from the unpleasantness of it, it's not likely to resolve the issue.

So which approach will be assertive, and make your point without causing a row? The answer is the third one. It puts the focus firmly on you and your feelings, rather than on your boss's behaviour, while still making the point. There's no hint of accusation in it; it's merely a statement of fact. For example: 'I feel frustrated when you check up on my work closely. I feel I'm not trusted to do a good job by myself.'

> **In their shoes**
>
> Your boss should realise that it's in their interests to know how you feel. If you're frustrated or angry or upset, they want to know about it. How else can they resolve it? And if they don't resolve it, they have someone on their team who is demotivated, demoralised, unhappy and not working as effectively as they might. If they want you to give your best work, they need to know about any negative feelings that are getting in your way.

Whenever you want to express your feelings, in a group meeting or one-to-one, use this approach. Focus on yourself and start by saying, 'I feel...when...' and take it from there. So long as you continue in the same vein, showing respect for the other person, there's no reason for a confrontation to develop. (For more long-term issues, you'll find this is also part of the feedback techniques explained in Chapter 9.)

Your boss may be in the habit of walking all over you. In this case, it may take them by surprise when you start to express how you feel. Or they may be used to you standing up to them, creating rows and being difficult to handle. Either way, they will find you far easier to work with once you adopt an assertive approach.

Be honest

You have a right to be honest. If you like, you can see this as a right to express your negative feelings as well as your positive ones. So if you disagree, or you don't want to do something, say so. If you think about this, it's much fairer towards your boss or whoever you're dealing with, too. Otherwise they will probably sense something is amiss but won't know what.

If you're going to be honest, don't beat about the bush – tell it straight. If you're not happy, say, 'I'm not happy.' If you disagree, say, 'I disagree.'

Don't confuse everyone and underrate the importance of your feelings by saying, 'Hmm, I'm not sure. I mean, I'm sure it's fine...it's just that...it's great, but...well, you know...' Spit it out and you'll achieve two benefits:

- Everyone will know what your point of view really is.

- You will have asserted clearly your right to say what you think or feel.

If your natural tendency is towards submissiveness, you will find it hard at first to state your opinions and feelings clearly. However, as soon as you try it you'll find it's really far easier than you think. If you're more prone to aggressive behaviour, you may be tempted to be honest to the point of being blunt, or even rude. This is something you have to watch out for, so pick your words carefully and express your feelings without upsetting or offending anyone.

This is easiest if you simply avoid emotive or negative words and stick to statements of fact. So instead of saying, 'That's rubbish,' say, 'I don't agree with that.' Instead of saying, 'I think we should scrap your idea,' say, 'I think we should reconsider.'

Mind your language

Assertive people use clear but constructive language, and look for phrases which encourage unity. They also remember that other people's views are as important as their own. So to be assertive you need to use expressions such as:
- I feel...
- I'd like to...
- Shall we...
- How about...
- What do you think?
- How do you feel?

Learn to stand your ground

As an assertive person, you should be able to fend off attempts to intimidate you, without becoming defensive and emotional. If your boss is inclined to bludgeon you, you need to learn how to assert your position without causing trouble. Don't be pressured into changing your opinion or putting up with something you're not happy with. There are two options for handling this kind of situation:

- State assertively how you feel. 'I'm not happy,' or 'I feel pressured.' This makes the position plain to your boss, and you can then follow the guidelines for expressing your feelings that we looked at earlier, or use the feedback techniques explained in Chapter 9.

- Adopt the 'stuck record' technique. This involves stating your position clearly and then repeating it as often as necessary. Don't become emotional or heated, just stick to your guns. For example: 'I don't feel ready to take on the scheduling on my own yet.' If your boss pressures you, repeat it: 'I need more training before I feel ready to take on the scheduling by myself.' Just carry on with this as long as you need to: 'I'm not happy about taking on the scheduling on my own. I need more training.' It's only a matter of time before your boss gets the point.

Look the part

Assertive body language will help to back up your assertive language. If you look nervous and submissive, this will send messages to your boss which contradict your words. The same goes for aggressive, overbearing posture. Assertive body language:
- is upright but relaxed
- doesn't impinge on the other person's personal space
- involves plenty of direct eye contact.

Be able to say 'no'

If you are under-assertive, you may well find it difficult to say no to people who ask you favours, especially your boss. There's the worry you might make them angry, or that they will dislike you or be disappointed in you. In fact, if you think about it, we all know plenty of people who are able to say no without losing popularity or respect, and without causing conflict.

If you avoid saying no, you find your workload slowly increasing, and you often take on tasks you're not happy to be doing. Some of us find a middle ground by saying no and lying about the reason – 'I can't do that, I'm afraid, I have an important meeting to go to.' This may get you off the hook, but it generally leaves you feeling uncomfortable, not to say worried that the other person will find out you've lied to them.

So the assertive answer is simply to say no when you want to. And again, this is actually fairer on the person you're dealing with. If they know you'll say no if you want to, they won't feel uncomfortable asking you to do things for them. If you start saying no to people, you may put yourself through agony the first couple of times trying to pluck up the courage, but once you've said it you usually find the other person thinks it's no big deal. 'OK, fair enough,' they reply, and cheerfully wander off to find another solution.

Here are a few tips for saying no:

- Remind yourself that you are quite entitled to say no, and there is no reason to feel guilty.

If you are under-assertive, you may well find it difficult to say no to people who ask you favours, especially your boss.

- It may help you to feel better to give a brief explanation of why you're saying no. You don't have to do this, but it can feel more co-operative. So rather than say, 'I don't have time to do that,' you may feel happier saying, 'I don't have time to do that – I'm already covering for Sandy this week.'

- You may also feel more helpful if you offer a different solution to their problem. For example, 'I don't have time to find the answer for you, but I can tell you where to find it yourself,' or 'I can't do it for you now, but if you can wait until Monday I'll be able to do it then.'

- If your boss is persistent, use the stuck record technique. Suppose your boss wants you to stay late: there's nothing in your contract that says you have to and on this occasion it would be really inconvenient, too. Just keep saying no until they get the message: 'I'm afraid I can't work late on Friday.' If your boss reiterates the request, reply, 'I'm sorry, but I can't work late on Friday. I have to take my mother to the hospital.' (You're not obliged to give a reason, but if you're happy to it often helps.) If they ask again, just keep telling them, 'I'm sorry, I can't do Friday.' Don't raise your voice or get upset – just be clear and assertive.

Practice makes perfect

If you have a repeated situation where you find it hard to be assertive, think through the assertive response and then rehearse it until you feel ready to put it into practice. Perhaps your boss persistently puts you down in meetings, or is always making unreasonable requests. Decide how you will handle it and run through the words until you feel comfortable with them. You could get a colleague or someone at home to roleplay it with you.

It's not easy to change personality overnight. If you're usually assertive, these guidelines will help you to become assertive more of the time. If, however, you are more often either submissive or aggressive, it will take you a little while to perfect the new, assertive you. And it will also take a while for people to notice the change. So don't expect other people's attitude towards you to change instantly. But give it time, and keep being assertive, and before long people will stop trying to walk all over you once they learn it doesn't work, or stop being defensive once they realise you are no longer aggressive.

8

How to listen...and be listened to

The idea of learning how to listen probably seems either unnecessary or patronising. Surely we've all been doing it since we were babies? Well, yes, we've all been listening superficially – that is to say, hearing. But really listening carefully is a different skill, and one which we can still learn after we've grown up. So what's the point of learning to listen properly? Well, it has several benefits:

- It prevents mistakes caused by crossed lines and poor communication.

- It helps you understand what is going on.

- It enables you to read between the lines when someone is speaking to you.

- It makes the other person feel more positively towards you.

So it's worth learning. Few of us are dreadful listeners (though we probably know one or two people who are), but most of us could listen better if we just learnt some of the basic techniques. Like so many other basic people skills, becoming a good listener is not only useful when you're dealing with your boss, but also when you're dealing with other people, from colleagues and subordinates to family and friends.

Two-way benefit

If you go through the motions of listening carefully, you'll find that without trying you really do listen better. Equally, if you listen carefully to begin with, you'll notice yourself following the guidelines in this chapter without even trying. Whether you approach this new set of skills by genuinely listening or by 'faking' it, you'll end up listening better than you did before. You can't lose.

Eliminate poor listening

To begin with, you need to do away with as many barriers to effective listening as you can. We all have them. There are times we listen better than others, and the worse times are generally the result of some block we have put up that inhibits our ability to listen properly. How many of these sometimes prevent you from listening as well as you might (be honest)?

- You're too busy planning your next response to take in what they're saying.

- You go off on a sidetrack train of thought sparked by something they said.

- You stop listening because you reckon you know what they're going to say.

- You are too preoccupied with thinking about how much you disagree to listen properly.

- You're simply listening out for an opportunity to butt in and say your piece.

- You get bored.

Once you learn to recognise these barriers when you put them up, it becomes much easier to take them down. So when you're listening to something you need to take in clearly, be conscious of any blocks you put up and simply remove them.

There's another set of barriers to good listening, and those are the ones that come from outside yourself. For example:

- You don't understand what the other person is saying – it's too complicated or they're using too much jargon.

- There are noises or distractions which are taking your attention.

- They are taking longer than you expected, and you're distracted because you're due in a meeting in two minutes.

- They are slow, long-winded, boring or rambling, or they keep repeating themselves.

Say that again?

Repetitious people can be very boring to listen to. But why do you think they repeat themselves? It's often because they don't think they're getting through to us. It's a vicious circle: they bore us so we don't listen, they sense we're not listening so they repeat themselves to get through to us, we become more bored...and so on. The solution is simple. If we listen properly in the first place, they'll have no need to repeat themselves, and everyone will benefit.

By and large, honesty is the best policy if you find you can't listen properly. For example:

- Tell the person you don't follow what they are saying. Ask them to explain it more clearly.

- Tell them if there are certain words you don't understand, and ask them to explain them to you.

- Let them know you are being distracted and ask to move somewhere where you can give them your full attention – it may be away from the door, or it might mean moving to another room.

- Explain that this is going to take longer than you thought, and you have to be somewhere else. Ask to get together later when you can concentrate better.

All these responses will actually flatter the person you're talking with, since they are all ways of telling them that you want the opportunity to listen to them better. If your boss wants you to take in what they're saying, they'll appreciate the fact that you clearly want to make the effort to listen fully.

The exception to the 'be honest' rule is when the problem is personal – your boss (or whoever you're dealing with) is boring, rambling or slow. In this case, it's not a good idea to say so straight out (no surprises there). By and large, you're just going to have to grin and bear it, and regard it as the ultimate training for good listening skills. However, you should find that when you practise effective listening, a lot of these barriers are partly removed or become easier to tolerate.

Listening actively

Once you've dealt with the barriers to listening, you can start actively listening to the other person. A large part of this entails concentrating on what they are saying, and making sure none of those barriers can pop up and get in the way. Catch yourself as soon as your mind starts to wander, or you find yourself planning your counter-argument, and bring your mind back to what the other person is saying to you.

Once you've dealt with the barriers to listening, you can start actively listening to the other person.

What's your point of view?

If you mentally view listening as an opportunity to improve your rapport with your boss (or whoever is speaking), and to learn or gather information, you'll find active listening far easier than if you view it as an opportunity to put your own point of view. A simple change of attitude can improve your listening skills vastly.

It's important to let the other person know you're listening. It helps them establish that they're making themselves clear. It is also polite and – when it comes to your boss – respectful. You'll also find that it's easier to concentrate and listen properly if you are focused on showing that you're listening. You can show your attention by various means:

- Making eye contact with the person who is speaking.

- Making encouraging noises, such as 'Mmm' or 'Uh-huh' or 'Go on...'

- Making encouraging signs, such as smiling, nodding or leaning forwards.

- Repeating back key phrases, such as 'Deliver by Tuesday week, OK'.

- Paraphrasing important points, such as 'So Richmond's can't go ahead with their launch unless we confirm the specifications this week.'

If you follow all these points you'll have to listen properly, and the other person will feel they have your full attention. In addition to making all these active indications that you're listening, there are also other things you need to avoid if you're going to listen fully. In particular, don't:

- interrupt (tempted though you may be)

- keep asking for minor points of clarification – save them until the other person has finished speaking.

See it their way

One useful technique is to make a conscious point of visualising what someone is telling you. If they are explaining that the pink copies go to the accounts department, conjure up a mental image of one of the desks in accounts covered in piles of pink paper. If they are giving you directions, create a picture in your mind of yourself turning left at a newsagent's, or right by a large tree, or whatever.

Silent signals

Some of the techniques for active listening involve using your body language to show that you're listening – nodding, making eye contact and so on. But listening fully also entails taking in the body language signals that your boss, or whoever you're talking to, is sending out – often unwittingly.

Our body language is almost always honest, unlike some of the words we use. I'm not calling your boss a liar, but we often say things we don't really mean, especially when it comes to talking about our feelings. We say things like, 'I'm not angry with you,' or 'I'm not worried' when in fact we are.

If you're attuned to body language as well as spoken words, you should be able to tell when the person you're listening to is saying one thing and indicating another with their body language. When this happens, you can bet it's the body language that is telling the truth. Often we sense that something doesn't ring true but we're not clear what. When this happens, analyse the body language and see if it's out of synch with the words.

Reading body language isn't a specialised science – it's just a matter of being on the lookout for the signals. Here are a few examples of mixed messages that should alert you to the possibility of an unspoken sub-text.

Words	Body language
'I'm confident we'll complete this project on time'	Strumming fingers, biting top lip
'I'm not angry'	Tense voice, leaning forward, clenching fist
'I'm really concerned to hear you're not happy'	Looking over your shoulder at something else, checking watch

I'm not suggesting that every one of these guarantees that your boss is lying to you. One or two minor contradictory actions or gestures may mean nothing. But a strong set of contradictions, especially coupled with a sixth sense on your part that what you're hearing doesn't ring true, is a good reason to suspect that you're not hearing the whole story.

Keep a weather eye on your skills

If you want to test how good you're getting at listening, here's a simple test you can do. Watch a three-minute weather broadcast, or listen to one on the radio, and see how much of it you can take in. Talk to the television if it helps, repeating back key phrases for example, and then see how much of the broadcast you can repeat back afterwards. You don't have to get the words exact, of course – the aim is to have absorbed the key points.

Getting other people to listen

If only everyone we deal with was as good at listening as they could be. And a boss who doesn't listen is often inclined to blame any lack of

A boss who doesn't listen is often inclined to blame any lack of communication on you rather than themselves.

communication on you rather than themselves. You'll find some specific tips on dealing with bosses who are bad listeners in the final part of this book. But here are some general pointers for getting the person you're talking to to listen properly:

- If you're talking to a poor listener, make sure you express yourself as succinctly and as briefly as you can. Make it as easy as possible for them to listen.

- Ask them to repeat key points to you: 'Can you say it back to me, just so I know I've made myself clear?' Often people can remember the last thing you said without having really taken it in; getting them to repeat it back will fix it more clearly in their mind.

- Ask them questions as you go along. Try to ask open questions (which can't be answered in a single word or two but require more thought). For example, if you're trying to tell your boss you haven't as much time as you feel you need for a project, you might ask, 'How would you tackle the research for this report with only a couple of days to do it in?'

Remember the written word

If you want people to remember what you've said to them, you don't have to rely wholly on their listening skills. Follow up important conversations with an email or memo summarising the key points.

If you follow all these guidelines you should find that active listening becomes a habit very quickly. And you'll soon get the hang of making poor listeners take more notice of what you're saying. So bad communication with your boss will become a thing of the past, you'll be clear what the unspoken messages are, and your boss will instinctively warm to you as someone who really takes notice of them.

9

How to use feedback techniques

Do you ever wish there was a non-confrontational, middle way between putting up with a situation you don't like or making a formal complaint about it? Either you let your boss demotivate and demoralise you, for example, or you go to their boss and make a big thing of it? Well, there is another way, and it's called feedback.

Feedback, broadly speaking, is information from other people on your performance. But there is also a technique known as feedback which is a more structured way of passing information between people. It is a form of general feedback, of course, but it has two useful characteristics in particular:

- It feeds information both ways between two people.
- It works especially well for resolving behavioural or personality difficulties.

Suppose your boss never sets you clear targets and then complains when you don't achieve what they expected of you. Or perhaps they never let you get a word in at meetings, so you wonder why you're even there. Or maybe they breathe down your neck all the time. Or they put you down in front of other people. Or every time they look over a piece of your work they make negative criticisms but never mention the good points.

The middle way

A feedback session is a more formal way of dealing with problems than a quick word when you pass in the corridor (as you'll see in a moment). This means that the boss has to recognise that this is a serious matter to you, and one which they must address. At the same time, however, it is not a formal meeting in which everything must be recorded – it is a private exchange between the two of you. So it doesn't carry any of the heavy implications of an official procedure such as a formal complaint.

Why feedback?

So what has feedback got that other techniques haven't?

- The big advantage of feedback is that it is non-confrontational. The technique is designed for you to be able to tackle tricky topics in a positive way, without either of you feeling the need to become defensive or aggressive.

- Another key advantage of feedback is that it's two-way. It may well be that the reason your boss constantly breathes down your neck, for example, is that you never give them progress reports or keep them in touch with how tasks are going. Often the kind of problem you would discuss at a feedback session has implications for both of you – understanding and action are needed on both sides to resolve the issue. Feedback encourages this two-way flow of dialogue.

- It's a technique which, once you've learnt it, you can apply to all sorts of knotty problems, from personality clashes to work-style conflicts. Its success rate is very high and, as an added reassurance, if your boss is so intractable that feedback doesn't achieve the result you want, at least it won't have made matters worse either.

Feedback gives you an easy outlet for those feelings before it's too late.

- Feedback is an ideal measure to use when things have reached the point where you feel you have to do something, but haven't yet reached the point where things have become unpleasant or drastic action is needed. In other words, you don't have to reach breaking point before you employ feedback. We often respond to frustrating or upsetting situations by bottling up our feelings until we blow, causing a scene and usually escalating the problem. Feedback gives you an easy outlet for those feelings before it's too late.

- Feedback techniques can be used for resolving specific, one-off issues, but they are also ideal for tackling persistent, longer-term problems.

Use it anywhere

This is a great way to resolve difficulties with your boss, but feedback techniques work just as well for resolving problems with colleagues or subordinates, or for bringing two subordinates together to resolve difficulties between themselves. (They also work, by the way, for resolving problems with friends and family away from work.)

Planning the meeting

Clearly, since the point of a feedback session is to be semi-formal and non-confrontational, you will need to arrange the session for a time when neither of you is rushed or excessively stressed, and when you can talk comfortably in privacy. Ideally, you want to arrange the following:

- a pre-arranged time when you both have at least half an hour to spare so you won't feel rushed

- no interruptions – that means a closed door and phone calls diverted or intercepted

- somewhere private to meet which should be in the office (not the pub), but which may well be neutral territory, such as a meeting room

- comfortable, informal and equal seating arrangements. Rather than facing each other across a desk, it's much better to sit at right angles to each other in comfortable chairs around a coffee table.

If as a boss you use feedback to deal with issues between you and a member of your team, make sure you follow these guidelines. However, where you're asking for a meeting with your own boss, you obviously won't always get the final say on where and when you meet. So the minimum you should (politely) insist on is:

- privacy without interruptions

- allocation of at least half an hour.

And how will you ask? The best approach is to say something like, 'I'd like to have a chat with you sometime. Please can we set up a time to meet, perhaps in one of the meeting rooms, for about half an hour?' If your boss asks what you want to talk about, it's best not to be too forthcoming or you'll find yourself having the session on the spot. So say, for example, 'I've been encountering a few problems lately in my work, and I'd like to see if you can help me resolve them.' If they push for you to be more specific about the problem, tell them, politely and assertively, 'I think it would be better to talk about it when we meet.'

Before the meeting takes place, think carefully through the key points you want to make, and how you are going to phrase them in a constructive and non-confrontational way (we'll look in more detail at how to phrase your comments in a moment). If you don't plan in advance, you may find yourself making matters worse by thoughtless wording of your remarks. Your boss may quite reasonably want some examples of the kind of behaviour you're talking about, so think through some appropriate instances you can quote.

Be prepared

Suppose you tell your boss that you feel humiliated when they criticise you in front of other people. Your boss replies, 'When have I ever done that?' You're going to feel pretty embarrassed when you can't come up with a single example. Don't forget that, until you're used to using feedback techniques, you may well feel nervous during the session, and this may prevent you remembering pertinent examples on the spot. So have them prepared in advance.

What to say

Once you're in the session, what are you going to say to your boss? Obviously, you need to start by telling them what the problem is. But focus on yourself, not them. Don't tell them the problem is that, 'You breathe down my neck all the time' – that would clearly rile them and lead to confrontation and argument. So start by saying, 'I feel...when you...'. For example, you might say, 'I feel I'm not trusted to do my job properly when you check up on me so often.'

Explain why this is a sufficient problem to warrant this conversation. For example, 'I feel demoralised because as well as feeling I'm not trusted, I also find it hard to feel satisfied with my performance; I feel I can't claim my achievements as my own when they've been so closely supervised.'

Once you've had your say, without being long-winded or repetitive, let your boss give their reaction – don't try to talk over them or prevent them getting a word in edgeways. And when they speak, listen to them properly (following the guidelines for positive listening from Chapter 8). They may ask you to give examples; in this case be ready to do so. They can't be expected to respond to a charge with no evidence, and they may need examples to clarify exactly what you mean.

Be prepared for the fact that your boss may give reasons for their behaviour which will be critical of your own work style. If you want them to treat your problems seriously without becoming defensive, you must do the same in return. They may tell you that they supervise you so closely because you never keep them in touch with your progress otherwise, or because you've been prone to make too many silly mistakes in the past. Hopefully, your boss will pick up on your tone and express these feelings as tactfully as you have done with yours. If they don't, however, you should do your best to take the remarks in good faith. If you react emotionally to a poorly worded criticism from your boss, you're not going to get this problem sorted.

In order to be constructive, and to keep things amicable, it also helps to point out occasions when your boss has behaved in a way you prefer. You might say, for example, 'I thoroughly enjoyed working on the presentation I gave to the conference last March. I felt you'd given me plenty of space to work in my own way, and I was very motivated by it. I feel very happy with that level of supervision.' This tells your boss clearly what kind of behaviour you would like from them.

If you react emotionally to a poorly worded criticism from your boss, you're not going to get this problem sorted.

> **No good points?**
>
> Even if your boss has never displayed the kind of behaviour you'd like them to, see if you can come up with examples of when they have acted at the better end of the scale, and let them know that this approach to you helps you feel better. It shows them what you're asking for, and it indicates that you're being reasonable and amicable.

If you've planned what you're going to say in advance, almost any boss will respond well to this kind of approach. You've been constructive, you've focused on yourself and not on them, and you've shown no animosity. You've simply asked them to help with a problem, and explained why it's worth resolving and how they can contribute. How can they argue with that?

So that's the opening stage of feedback: tell the boss how you feel, with examples if they ask, and listen while they reply. Let them know when they have behaved in the way that you prefer, both to indicate a constructive attitude on your part and to illustrate exactly what you're asking for.

The next stage of feedback is to find a solution to the problem, but first it's worth looking at the best way to express yourself to keep the session positive and friendly.

How to express yourself

We've already seen that it's important to focus on yourself, and to start sentences with, 'I feel…when you…' rather than, 'You make me feel…' Here are some more tips for putting your comments in a friendly and non-confrontational way.

- Avoid provocative expressions such as 'you breathe down my neck' or 'you bully me'.

- Don't exaggerate. If your boss sometimes lets you get on with tasks unsupervised, for example, they will wonder why they bother if you tell them, 'You always supervise me more closely than necessary' (let alone, 'You're always breathing down my neck').

- Don't judge. It's not for you to tell your boss that they're not a good manager, or that they're useless with people. (If you use feedback with colleagues or subordinates, it's equally important to follow this rule.) More to the point, it's not helpful and it will turn the session into an argument instead of a constructive means of resolving a tricky issue.

- Don't label your boss. Remarks like 'You're negative' or 'You're a control freak' aren't helpful. These remarks are easier to avoid if you focus on your boss's *behaviour*, rather than on what they *are*.

Take your time

Don't be embarrassed to take time choosing your words. Your boss will recognise that you are making an effort to be constructive, and will respond in kind. Far better to pause while you pick the right word than to come out with the wrong one and risk offending or insulting your boss.

Getting results

You've outlined the problem to your boss, and heard their response. Now you've both had a chance to discuss the issue, it's time to look for a solution. Feedback, after all, is an eminently practical technique, focused on putting things right.

The first thing to do is to suggest a solution. You may have one pre-pared in advance, but your boss's comments may mean that it needs adapting. You'll want to demonstrate a spirit of compromise, so be prepared to give some ground. It's no good suggesting to the boss, 'How about this? I'll carry on exactly as before, and you change your behaviour totally. That should work.' Sure, in an ideal world it would probably work very well for you. But how would you like it if someone else suggested it to you? If you ask them to make all the running, you're implying they are totally responsible for the problem. Now, true or not, that's not a helpful implication.

Offering a compromise implies accepting a shared responsibility. So you might suggest, 'If I were to give you regular progress reports, say once a week, would you feel able to supervise me less closely?' Once you've made your suggestion, let them respond so you can gauge how they feel about it. No solution is going to work unless you are both behind it, so their view is as important as yours. You need their full agreement to any proposal before it's worth adopting it.

They may agree to your suggestion straight away – and if you've been listening to them properly you're more likely to come up with a solution they find workable. Or they may have an alternative to offer: 'I'd prefer it if you came to me to ask for advice or help when you run into problems; then I'd feel confident in letting you work unsupervised knowing you'd ask for support when you needed it.' It's only right you should treat their proposed solution as seriously as you want them to treat yours. So don't pooh-pooh any idea, however daft you think it sounds; simply explain why you don't feel it would resolve the problem.

Discuss all the suggestions on the table until you arrive at a solution that you both feel will work. One of you should then recap to be sure you've both agreed to the same thing. Your boss, as the senior of you, may choose to do this but, if they don't volunteer a recap, do it your-

No solution is going to work unless you are both behind it, so their view is as important as yours.

self. You may well also want to agree a follow-up meeting in a few weeks to review how the new system is working out.

And that's feedback. A simple way to resolve shared problems that doesn't lead to arguments or dissent. A two-way approach that leaves you both feeling you've gained from the discussion.

Ten steps to feedback

Just to summarise, here are the key steps to holding a productive and effective feedback session:

1. Arrange a meeting in advance which is private, uninterrupted and gives you plenty of time to talk.
2. Think through the key points you want to make, and how you will phrase them. Get examples ready in case your boss asks for them.
3. Tell the boss what the problem is, starting your explanation, 'I feel...when you...'. Explain why this is such a problem. Give them examples if they ask for them.
4. Listen (properly) while your boss replies, and be prepared to take any negative comments on board.
5. Give your boss examples of times they have exhibited the kind of behaviour you prefer.
6. Pick your words carefully. In particular, avoid provocative expressions, exaggeration, judging or labelling.
7. Once the issue has been clearly outlined, from both points of view, offer a solution that takes your boss's comments into account.
8. Be prepared to compromise; if you both give some ground neither of you will come away feeling short-changed.
9. When you have discussed the options, agree a solution that suits you both and recap to make certain you're both clear about what action you'll take.
10. Set a follow-up session for a few weeks ahead to review your joint progress.

PART

III

How to manage a difficult boss

Not many of us are lucky enough to have perfect bosses, and if you were one of the few I don't imagine you'd be reading this book. If you've been following everything you've read so far, you've done all the work you reasonably can on your own performance and behaviour. Any outstanding problems aren't realistically going to be down to you.

Let's face it, bosses are only human (at best). Most of them have a few faults, and some of them have bucketloads. So how are you going to handle the characteristics that make your boss difficult to work with? What you need is a troubleshooter's guide to handling the key types of problem boss, from the one who never listens to the type who always takes credit for *your* ideas.

10

Tricky bosses

So here it is. Twenty-five different tricky characteristics and how to handle them. You'll probably recognise a fair few, and your boss may even exhibit more than one, I'm afraid.

The boss who...

...never listens

This is infuriating. You know they're not taking in what you're saying, but you don't feel you can start screaming, 'Listen to me, dammit!' at your boss without jeapordising your position. It's not just that they're being rude – it can also lead to serious problems. For example, you tell them about an issue you have to deal with and what you intend to do about it, and they reply, 'Mmm-hmm. OK.'

In fact, they've taken nothing in and three weeks later they demand to know why you made a major decision alone when you should have consulted them. It's no use telling them you *did* consult them – they will insist you didn't and they really won't remember that you did. How can they remember something they never registered in the first place?

So what can you do? Here are the best ways to get your boss to take in and absorb what you're saying:

- Ask them to repeat back what you've just said. You won't want to say, 'I don't reckon you've been listening to a word I've said,' so instead try a tack such as, 'I'm not sure I've explained it clearly. Could you just repeat it back for me?' In order to do this, they will have to take note of what you just said.

- Another way to achieve the same effect is to ask open questions (ones which don't allow a yes/no answer), so they can't simply mumble 'Mmm' at you absently. In the case of checking a decision with them, for example, don't just present them with your decision and the reasons behind it. Fill them in on the facts and present them with a choice of decisions and make them choose. If they choose the wrong one without thinking it through properly, you've now engaged them sufficiently to discuss the comparative merits of the two options with you.

- If by any chance the boss does this with no one else, or only a few others, you'll need to address the possibility that you're adding to the problem. People who don't listen are especially inclined to switch off with people who don't get to the point quickly. If this could be you, prepare anything important you need to say to them so that you can put it as briefly and succinctly as possible.

- Get it in writing. Email your comments, briefings or requests to them. Not only can they not deny that you've discussed the thing with them, they may well respond better to this medium, and give you the responses you want.

Don't take it personally

Try to bear in mind – for your own sanity – that most people who don't listen are unaware of the fact. It's not malice, or even lack of concern about you and your work. They almost certainly do it to everybody. You just need to be smarter than your colleagues about handling it.

...never communicates

Poor communicators can cause all sorts of trouble. And when it's your boss who's failing to communicate, the results can be devastating. If you don't have the necessary information, it's almost impossible to do your job properly. And it's demoralising, too. It's hard to stay motivated and keen when no one seems to think you important enough to be told what's going on.

You can certainly use feedback techniques (Chapter 9) on an uncommunicative boss, and if they are seriously deficient in the communication department you'll probably have to. But many bosses are uncommunicative enough to be tricky without necessarily warranting major action. Often a few simple strategies will remedy the problem.

- A lot of the time, you've got a pretty clear idea what you're not being told. Assuming your boss isn't deliberately withholding information, they probably haven't realised that you need this information too. They just don't think. Often, all you need to do is ask. So when they ask you to do a task, say, 'Sure. Can you tell me what it's for, and when it's needed by?' Or when you need to know what's going on, ask, for example, 'I've heard that one of our major customers is about to call in the receivers. Is it true, and how will it affect us?'

- Make a point of asking open rather than closed questions of them as a matter of course. So instead of asking, 'Will we be discussing the new software at Monday's meeting?' (to which they can simply reply, 'yes'), ask them, 'What aspects of the new software will we be discussing on Monday?' They'll have to give you a fuller answer.

- If your boss is one of those introvert, quiet types who never thinks that you might need information, they may well simply not reply to some of your questions. When faced with this kind of person we often make things harder for ourselves: as soon as there's a silence we fill it, thereby letting them off the hook. This perpetuates their behaviour. To avoid this, ask a question and then shut up until they answer – eventually the silence will become so uncomfortable that even they will notice, and give you a reply. This technique works with anyone, but it's great with bosses because it's perfectly polite. You've asked the question so the onus is clearly on them, and not you, to speak next.

- Some bosses withhold information deliberately, sad to say, as some kind of power game. They feel important because they know something you don't. Petty, huh? This is a different type of behaviour, and you'll find it dealt with further on, under 'the boss who is secretive'.

...never does anything

You'll never turn this boss into a powerhouse of frantic activity, so there's no point wasting your efforts trying to. What you need to do is to eliminate the negative effect on you. The problems arise when you don't get the information, resources or decisions you need to get on with your own job effectively. So address these issues, and leave your boss to twiddle their thumbs or chase their tail – whichever variation on doing nothing is their personal preference.

No change there

It's a general rule of thumb with tricky bosses – and tricky people of any kind – that you'll never change their personalities. You'll only drive yourself crazy in the attempt. So don't aim to turn your boss into someone they're not – just find techniques that help you cope comfortably with them the way they are.

Some bosses withhold information deliberately, sad to say, as some kind of power game.

- This boss isn't deliberately withholding support (later on we'll look at bosses who won't back you up). They are just so ineffectual or incompetent that they never get round to giving you what you need when you need it. The answer is to do it for yourself. You have to do their job for them, in order to be able to do your own. This may sound unfair on you and your workload – that's because it is. But it's a great deal more productive in the long run than waiting for support that never materialises. And this kind of boss will probably be grateful that you've taken a task off their hands – if they even notice.

- The trick is to anticipate the problem and do what needs doing in plenty of time. This will ease the pressure on you enormously, and enable projects to run smoothly.

- If your boss will let you get away with it, offer to elicit information from their fellow managers yourself. If they feel you're treading on their toes, send them a memo or an email listing precisely what you need to know, and by when. This makes it far easier for them to get around to finding out information for you.

- When it comes to decisions or resources, write a brief report or proposal for them, justifying what resources you need, or recommending a particular decision. Once you've done all the work, they might as well get on with the easy bit of passing your brief, report or proposal on for approval. They can always take the credit by claiming they asked you to put the material together.

- It's generally better not to offer to do this kind of work for your boss – just present your paperwork as a *fait accompli*. If you offer they often refuse, convinced they'll get around to it themselves...and then they don't. Just hand it over, saying, 'I thought you might find this useful.'

...is secretive

This kind of deliberate withholding of information is a power game some bosses play. It makes them feel important knowing that they know something you don't. The straightforward way to counter this is to make them feel important without having to keep secrets (much as it may stick in your craw).

- Be deferential to this kind of boss, without crawling. Just make sure you always show them respect, so they know you are aware they are senior to you. Don't try to get too familiar with them; they won't like it. The more they feel their importance is recognised, the less they will need to play this kind of game.

- Be very specific about what information you need from them, and ask for it in a way that acknowledges that they know something you don't. For example, 'I really can't prepare this material without knowing precisely what the customer is looking for, and I reckoned if anyone knows the answer it'll be you.' (Don't get too creepy about this, but you get the picture.) The point is that you're letting them know they've achieved their aim – being recognised as the one who holds the power – so now they can afford to pass on the information.

...is prejudiced

When people judge you wrongly for something you have no control over, it is extremely frustrating. When it's your boss, it can also damage your career. Whether they are sexist, racist, ageist or classist – or anything else – you need to tackle the problem.

Feedback can work extremely well for this problem, forcing your boss to acknowledge that your performance is not affected by your age, gender, race or any other similar factor. But alongside this, there are a couple of other steps you can take to help your case.

Force of numbers

You may not be the only member of your team the boss is prejudiced towards. If several of you have the same problem, sound out the others and see if they also want to take action. If you all decide that you want the problem resolved without making a formal complaint or a big issue, you can all follow the suggestions below. A joint feedback session can make the point firmly, but be aware that if the boss feels threatened or intimidated you could make matters worse, so get everyone to follow the guidelines carefully for using feedback without becoming confrontational.

- Don't get involved in an argument with your boss about their prejudice. Decline to discuss whether women are better than men, whether experience or youth is better, and so on. You will only reinforce their prejudice. You're not going to change your mind after such a debate, and it's no more likely they will.

- Show by example. Make sure that you don't reinforce their ideas. Volunteer for tasks which will prove your point, and behave in ways which will undermine their prejudice. For example, if your boss is a sexist woman who thinks all men are dunderheads, take on a task requiring delicate diplomacy when you get the chance, and let her see you can handle it. If you're a lot older than your boss, don't be a stick-in-the-mud, but let them see that older people can be creative and open to new ideas. When you decide to ask for a feedback session with your boss, you'll be armed with examples that contradict their prejudice.

- At the same time, don't inadvertently reinforce their views. If you're a woman with a sexist boss, don't ask him to change the light bulb for you. It may not have anything to do with your ability to do the job, but it will convince him women are pathetic – even if you were asking only because he's six inches taller than you. You don't want to arm your boss with examples to use at the feedback session. When you ask for examples of how your work is detrimentally affected by your being a woman/being over 50/being public school-educated/being black/being gay or whatever your boss's prejudice is, you want them to be unable to cite any example.

Of course, you always have the option here of going to your boss's boss with a complaint (or even taking more extreme legal action if you believe you have a case). Feedback is always worth trying first, but if your boss is unresponsive is it worth going over their head? Only you can decide on the answer to this, but here are a few factors to take into account:

- Is your boss's boss likely to be sympathetic – or if not is there a personnel department which you could go to instead?

- How is your boss likely to respond? Their boss can't do anything useful without talking to them, so it's no good thinking they won't find out. Is it likely to pull them up short, or more likely to make them resentful towards you?

- Have you any firm evidence of their treating you in a prejudiced fashion? If not, you have relatively little chance of success unless you encounter someone sympathetic who knows your boss well enough to know you're being honest.

- Do you have colleagues who will vouch for the prejudiced treatment you say you've been receiving from your boss?

- How much do you want this job? I'm not suggesting you should say nothing, but the action you take may be affected by your answer to this question. If the job's become unbearable, you might as well take drastic action since you have nothing to lose. If the reaction makes things worse, you'll be happy to leave. But if you thoroughly enjoy the job apart from your boss's attitude, you'll want to try more circumspect approaches first.

...is a perfectionist

We should all aim for perfection every time in our work, and having a perfectionist for a boss shouldn't be a problem. But, in fact, so-called perfectionists are rarely perfect. They aim for top quality, but forget that there are other vital factors too, such as time. Delivering a job that is spot-on but a week late is not perfection. This is your problem. Your boss wants not only perfection, but also perfection in an unreasonable length of time, or at an unreasonable cost.

- Point out to your boss when they set you a task that they are asking for the impossible. Tell them, 'I can do that to the standard you want, but not by Tuesday. If you want it then, I'll have to compromise else-where.' Get them to recognise the problem in advance and help find a workable solution, rather than waiting until afterwards to com-plain that the brief was impossible.

- As well as the problem of asking for the impossible, some perfec-tionist bosses expect you never to make a mistake. If you suffer under this kind of boss, you'll need to use feedback, explaining that you feel under undue pressure to be superhuman, and that you need to be allowed to learn from your mistakes sometimes.

Aim for perfection yourself

You'll get on best with a perfectionist boss if you make sure your work is never slapdash or shoddy, and that you genuinely *do* learn from your mis-takes. If you deliver poorly prepared work, or repeat your mistakes, you have only yourself to blame when you meet trouble from the boss.

Your boss wants not only perfection, but also perfection in an unreasonable length of time, or at an unreasonable cost.

...is unorganised

If you're unorganised yourself, you may not mind working with this kind of boss. But if you're highly organised they will drive you to distraction. They won't be able to find the information you need, they will forget to turn up to meetings, they'll promise you something and then disappear without sorting it out.

The one good thing to be said for most unorganised bosses is that they know their failings, and they are usually happy for you to do some of their organising for them. So long as you don't blatantly tread on their toes or play the moral superior, you shouldn't fall out with them.

- You're going to have to do some of the work yourself. Create systems if you need them – but make them idiot-proof if you expect your boss to stick to them. Remind them in advance about meetings and appointments, and chase them up for information they've promised *before* they miss the deadline they promised it by. For example, 'You are still going to be able to get me those figures by the end of the day, aren't you, so I can finalise my report?'

- Make sure your boss understands why you need them to turn up to meetings, give you information or stick to the system. Make them aware of the potentially damaging consequences of their disorganisation: 'If I don't get the pink copies from you within 24 hours, the deliveries go out late and we start getting customer complaints.' Or, 'If you don't give me the mail before 4 o'clock, I can't get through it in time to knock off at 4.30. That means I'm late to pick the kids up from school.'

- Unless you're a secretary or PA, don't try to overhaul your boss completely – it will be a full-time job in itself. Just concentrate on those areas which interfere with your own job, and learn to leave your boss to their own devices the rest of the time.

...is no good at their job

Bosses who are downright incompetent can make your life immensely difficult. Often their inability to do the job also mutates into one of the other problems in this chapter (passing the buck, for example, being unorganised, or taking credit for your ideas).

The incompetence itself is a problem when it reflects on you. The whole department performs poorly and you (and your team mates) miss out on bonuses, promotions and successes. The challenge is to make sure that others realise that you don't deserve to be tarred with the same brush as your boss.

Get out

If your boss is incompetent, your aim should be to get promoted out of this department as soon as possible – or promoted into your boss's job. However, you don't want to make your boss feel threatened, or you will make a bad situation worse. So don't start trying to steal their job. It's only a matter of time before they move (or get moved) without your help, especially once you've made sure everyone knows that it's not you (and your colleagues) who is incompetent.

- Get as much of your own contribution to the organisation down in writing as you can. Instead of taking ideas to the boss verbally, write them down as proposals. These may only be a page long, but they're there in black and white. Now make sure they get seen outside the department. Copy them to anyone you can justify copying them to. You can tell your boss, 'I've copied this to despatch because I thought their input would be useful in helping us to schedule,' or, 'I thought Mike could use this idea in his department, too, so I've emailed him a copy of my proposal.'

- Now do the same with any warnings you have to make. If you are concerned that a project is going off-course, email your boss or send them a memo outlining your concerns and your recommendations for remedying the problem. Again, copy them wherever you can. Even if you can't, at least keep your own copies. Then when things go wrong, it will be clear it wasn't your fault. In fact, if the boss had listened to you, they wouldn't have gone wrong. And suppose the boss *does* take your advice? Better still – you have a success on your hands, and the paperwork shows it was all thanks to your intervention.

- Finally, get your achievements down in black and white, and circulated as widely as possible. You don't have to send round a memo saying, 'Aren't I brilliant? Look what I did.' You could email your boss with essential details of a big new contract you've just landed and copy it to other relevant departments. Just make sure it's clear that you were the one who landed the deal, came up with the idea or put in the hard work.

...passes the buck (on to you)

None of us likes being blamed at the best of times, and being blamed for someone else's mistakes is particularly galling. But it's something certain bosses do. It's bad enough when they salve their own conscience by pointing the finger at you in private, but blaming you publicly for their mistakes simply can't be permitted. It can be deeply damaging to your career.

- For a start, if your boss makes a habit of this, use the same techniques as you would with a boss who is no good at the job. That way your real achievements are down in writing for when you need them – appraisals, promotion interviews and so on. If your boss tries to blame you in private, draw their attention to the relevant paperwork.

- Encourage your boss to put instructions to you in writing. If you encounter problems with this, simply email them saying, for example, 'Before I launch into this, can I clarify your instructions? You've asked me to...'; they need only send back an email saying, 'Yes' to have committed themselves on paper.

- Don't try to put the blame back on your boss, realistic though it might seem. If you say, 'It wasn't my fault, it was yours, and I can prove it' you may make your point, but you'll do serious damage to your working relationship. Your boss probably knows perfectly well it was their fault – that's why they're so desperate to palm the blame off on to you. Instead, use the word 'we' a lot, as in, 'We certainly didn't get the results we wanted...', or, 'With hindsight, we'd have done better to set the schedule further in advance...' and then focus on solutions. Don't accept the blame, just aim to avoid pointing fingers, and move on to the next stage.

- If your boss blames you for their mistakes in public, don't try to pass the blame back to them in front of everyone else. It may be fair, but it won't work. Most people won't be able to tell which of you is telling the truth, and the result will be that you'll look petty and your boss will be furious with you. Instead, take the blame, but do it collectively, using that word 'we' a lot: 'There's no denying we misjudged this one...'

- Now focus on the solution, outlining how you think the problem can be solved, and what you can do to help. Drop the 'we' for this bit, and talk about yourself as 'I' when it comes to finding solutions and rescuing disasters.

...is a poor motivator

When there's no recognition, enthusiasm or reward coming back from your boss, you wonder why you bother making an effort at work. Some of these bosses show little or no interest in your work whatever you do, while others wield plenty of sticks but no carrots – if you don't pull your weight they'll soon make you feel bad about it, but do your best and you won't even get a thank you.

Living with it

You'll have to accept that some bosses just aren't the type to become the world's greatest motivators. There are steps you can take, but they will only get you so far – in the end you must compromise, and accept that until you or the boss moves on, you're going to have to live with less recognition than you deserve. Take comfort from the fact that your non-expressive boss may actually think the world of you – they just don't think to say so, or perhaps don't know how to say so.

- Try feedback (see Chapter 9) with this boss. It won't suddenly get you a hundred thank-yous a day, but it may well have some effect. And one word of encouragement a week from this boss will mean as much as one every hour from some others. If your boss is unaware of this problem, they may well take on board any feelings and comments you express during a feedback session.

- You could try asking for more frequent performance reviews and feedback sessions after you complete projects. If you've done a good job, it's hard for them not to say so in this situation. And most of these bosses aren't trying to avoid motivating you; they simply don't realise the effect their natural reticence is having. Asking specifically for their view of your performance should earn you any recognition you deserve.

- Ask for rewards in advance. For example, 'If this presentation goes well, could I run the next presentation myself?' or, 'If I exceed my

One word of encouragement a week from this boss will mean as much as one every hour from some others.

target this quarter, will it be reflected in my next bonus?' I know it's not as good as a reward spontaneously offered, but you have to meet this boss half way.

- Learn to translate any recognition into normal language. When your boss says, 'Good,' you need to hear, 'Terrific work! Well done!'

- Find ways to motivate yourself. Work towards targets of your own, or promise yourself a reward for certain achievements. Or aim towards promotion or earning new responsibilities as an incentive to keep you enthusiastic. Presumably your team members have the same problem, so perhaps you could find collective incentives. You could try friendly competition, or set yourself team targets and agree that you'll all go out for an evening together if you meet them. Or simply make a point of congratulating each other on good work, even if the boss doesn't join in.

...throws tantrums

This kind of behaviour is abusive, and there's no reason why you have to stand for it. Your assertiveness skills (see Chapter 7) will serve you well here – you'll need them. If you're a parent you'll have some experience of dealing with tantrums, no doubt, and you'll know that the first rule of handling a tantrum is never give in to it.

There's no reason to think that your boss's tantrum is any different from the kind of tantrum a small child throws. In fact, they've probably been doing it since they were a small child. Why? Because they've found it works. So the key to handling it is to teach them that it doesn't work, at least not with you. Never give in to it.

- Don't respond to a tantrum with emotion. Remain cool and rational, and stick to facts (if you get a word in at all). Set them an example of adult behaviour. If there's anyone else around you'll look good and the boss will look extremely foolish.

> ## Who are you working for?
>
> When your boss throws tantrums, you need to be assertive and recognise that just because this person is your boss, they have no right to treat you in this abusive way. If they have chosen to behave like a small child, they have also chosen – whether they recognise it or not – to suspend their authority over you temporarily. You don't work for a small child, you work for a rational adult. You have to deal with them only in their adult mode.

- Don't give in to them when they're having a tantrum. Let them see that their behaviour gets them nowhere and makes them look very foolish. Eventually they'll learn there's no point in it.

- Any time you decide you've had enough, you're entitled to leave. You can either make an excuse ('I've got another meeting at 10.00') or simply say, 'I'm here to do a job, not to be shouted at. I'm going to leave and I'll discuss this with you when you're calm.' Now go. Don't be lured back or drawn into any further 'discussion'. They won't like it, but they can hardly sack you – or even complain to *their* boss about you – for refusing to be abused. If you use this technique every time, they'll have to learn to deal with you rationally.

- If you can, enlist the support of your colleagues. If everyone in the team adopts this approach, it will work much faster.

If your boss has been throwing tantrums to good effect for 30 or 40 years, they're not going to be able to give it up in a matter of days. So you need to accept that this is a long-term process. However, the techniques above will work in the end (though the tantrums may continue towards other people who aren't as smart as you). In the meantime, you'll find them easier to handle, and you can leave if they get unpleasant.

...humiliates you in public

This boss puts you down in public, making snide or sarcastic remarks, and does their best to belittle you in front of other people. If you are the only person they do this to, you would also do well to look at 'the boss who...picks on you personally' later in this chapter. But even if they do it to many of their subordinates, that's little comfort.

The trick is to turn their technique back on themselves, by behaving rationally and reasonably in a way which makes them look small. Here's how it's done.

- To start with, don't give them any ammunition. If they are sarcastic about the standard of your work, make sure it's always excellent. If they are snide about you turning up late, get to meetings on time. You can't win with these bosses unless their remarks are unjustified.

- If you want to, you can ignore the remarks with dignity. But this won't stop them. On the other hand, if you get riled you simply find yourself rowing with your boss, which helps no one.

- So the logical middle way is to be assertive. Remain calm and unflustered, but ask them to justify their remarks. When they snidely say, 'Another day off work again yesterday, I notice' reply with, 'Apart from taking a day off a fortnight ago for a family funeral, I don't remember taking a day off for several months. Which occasions are you referring to?' This is an entirely reasonable response, but will leave them looking pretty foolish. The more you do it, the sooner they will learn it's not wise to try to humiliate you in public. Teach the technique to your colleagues too.

Remain calm and unflustered, but ask them to justify their remarks.

Don't change the record

If your sarcastic boss is hard to handle, you may need to take the technique one step further. If you ask them, 'When did I last take a day off work?' they may either laugh off your response or give a general answer, such as, 'I can't remember, it happens so often.' Don't stand for this. Adopt the stuck record technique and put pressure on them to answer the question: 'No, seriously. I don't believe I've taken a day off for over six months. Tell me when you think I've taken time off.' You may never get a straight answer, but repeating the question once or twice will make your point clearly enough that they'll feel uncomfortable. After they've experienced this a few times, they'll think twice before throwing out unfounded negative remarks.

...won't back you up

It is a manager's job to make sure everyone in their team is able to do their job as well as possible. That means giving you all the support you need in terms of resources, training and so on. It is also their job to take responsibility for the whole department. Any mistake you make is ultimately their mistake, because they didn't equip you to prevent it happening.

The good boss gives you everything you need to do your job, and then carries the can if anything goes wrong. But not all bosses are that good. Some of them give you little or no support, and then step back when things go wrong, leaving the full spotlight to fall on you.

- These two problems are linked because it is often the same type of boss who commits both crimes – lack of support and unwillingness to share responsibility. They are also linked because if you were to get the support you needed in the first place, you would rarely make mistakes, so your boss's readiness to point the finger at you would rarely matter.

- You need to spell out for this boss exactly what you need from them. Tell them, for example, you'll need them to elicit co-operation from the marketing department, with access to their records, and you'll need to be allowed to devote a day a week to this project if it's to be completed on time. And you'll need to be trained in using the software before you can start. In order to get what you need from this boss you'll have to be specific right from the start, so they have no excuses.

- Let them know why you need these things. Explain that if you don't the project will go over budget, or not be finished on time, or you'll be unable to do it to standard. If they think you're asking too much they'll have to hammer it out with you now, rather than simply fail to come up with the goods.

- Put this list of requirements down in writing for them – email will do. That way it's down on paper, and they can't claim they didn't know what your needs were. Include any time constraints; for example, 'I need this information by Friday 10th in order to complete the project in time for the new product launch.'

- Having elicited their agreement by this means, you should continue to email or send written reminders every time some promised resource fails to materialise, including a reminder of the consequences if you don't get what you need by the agreed time.

- If things still go wrong, and your boss attempts to let you take the blame, you're now in a position to demonstrate that it wasn't your fault. Your paperwork shows that you weren't given what you needed when you needed it, and that your boss knew it.

- Now you can respond in the way outlined earlier for 'the boss who...passes the buck'.

> **The sad thing is that people who aren't allowed to develop get fed up and tend to leave eventually.**

...won't let you develop

The longer you do your job, the easier it gets. It stands to reason. So now you want new challenges and fresh responsibilities. But your boss is happy for you to stay as you are, doing a good job and not likely to need a lot of input or to make any significant mistakes. Training up staff is a lot more time-consuming, not to mention riskier, for a boss than leaving them where they are – or so the boss thinks.

The sad thing is that people who aren't allowed to develop get fed up and tend to leave eventually (which actually costs the boss more in the long run). But you'd rather not leave. If you were only allowed to develop, you'd be very happy in this job. So what can you do?

Speedy development

Try feedback (Chapter 9) on a boss who won't let you develop. Once you've explained to your boss how frustrated you're feeling, they may well co-operate. The feedback technique is great because it's non-confrontational, and this is just what you need to encourage your boss to help. It avoids the temptation to threaten them ('If you don't let me develop my skills I'll hand in my notice'). Threatening is never helpful, as it simply riles your boss.

- Volunteer for extra responsibilities as often as you can, and ask for training and new responsibilities. In particular, point out to your boss the advantages to them. For example, 'If I spent a day or two with Sonia learning how to organise conferences, I could cover for her when she's on holiday, and I'd know exactly what I was doing.'

As you can see, this approach should reassure your boss that there will be less risk training you than leaving you untrained.

- If your boss is reluctant to let you develop because they are a control freak, see the section later in this chapter on handling the control freak boss.

...is negative

The negative boss always looks on the pessimistic side of things. They tell you your ideas won't work, and their outlook is always bleak. This has two key disadvantages. First, it's demoralising to work in a negative atmosphere. And second, it's particularly demotivating to have your own ideas and suggestions criticised and often dismissed.

So why is your boss so negative? It's almost always down to a fear of failure. If you're prepared for the worst, it won't come as a shock (goes the thinking). And if you never take risks, you won't make big mistakes. Of course, this is a nonsense since its logical conclusion is total inaction, and the potentially huge mistake of missing opportunities. But that's not how your boss sees it.

- Remember that without any negative input, failure would be far more frequent. In moderation, negative comments are a helpful way of spotting pitfalls in time to avoid them. So don't dismiss all negativity out of hand – aim to tone it down, not eliminate it.

- As far as general negativity is concerned, you need to get your boss to be specific. When they tell you 'It will never work', ask them which aspects of the project won't work, and why. This ensures at least that they focus on rational worries, even if they have them out of proportion.

- Now play on your boss's fear of failure. Point out why rejecting your idea would be riskier than accepting it: 'If we don't take the initiative, our competitors will and we'll be left behind', or, 'On average, each member of this team generates twice as much income as they cost the organisation. So if we don't take on two more people, we could be losing the department something like £50,000 a year.'

...is a bully

This kind of boss sometimes exhibits several of the characteristics we're looking at in this chapter. They may throw tantrums, humiliate you and pick on you, as well as being unreasonable, pressuring you to work long hours and otherwise behaving abusively.

Working for a bully can be extremely stressful. Some bosses resort to bullying when they're under pressure, while others bully constantly. Some bully everyone, while others bully only one or two team members. Whichever type your boss is, here are a few strategies for handling them.

- Try feedback (Chapter 9). It can be scary when you have a bully for a boss, but it's more likely to work than anything else. If you're diplomatic, there's no reason why the meeting should make matters worse, and it's often helpful. Let your boss know how their behaviour makes their department less effective (which will obviously reflect on them). You can do this non-confrontationally by saying something like, 'I find it very hard to perform as well as I could when I feel under excessive pressure, and my morale – and the morale of those who work closely with me – suffers as a result.'

- Practise your assertiveness skills (Chapter 7) until you can stand up for yourself in front of your boss without becoming confrontational. Once their bullying tactics stop working on you, they will be less inclined to use them.

- If these techniques don't elicit the results you need, and you feel the problem warrants further action, make a formal complaint against your boss. Before you do this, however, collect as much evidence as you can, enlist the support of witnesses, keep a log of your boss's bullying behaviour, and keep copies of any memos or emails which contain bullying language. Some organisations now have an anti-bullying policy; if yours does you can refer to this for advice on how to complain.

When all else fails...

In the last resort, you may be able to take legal action against your bully of a boss. However, be prepared for the fact that you will probably have to leave your job first so that you can claim constructive dismissal, so take legal advice before you do anything.

...picks on you personally

Maybe your boss is a great boss to most of the team, but not for you. Being singled out and picked on is deeply distressing; arguably worse than receiving the same treatment from a boss who dishes it out to everybody. What can you do when you're being victimised?

- Talk to your colleagues if you can. See if they are aware of your problem, and enlist their support if possible. If they back you up when the boss is picking on you, it will make it obvious that they can see what the boss is up to – which may act as a deterrent.

- Talk to your boss. Use feedback techniques, and try to find out why they're picking on you. Don't put it in these terms; instead tell them you get the feeling that they are displeased with something you're doing, or failing to do. Ask them what you can do to resolve things. If there's a specific cause, the boss will probably tell you in response to this and you can take steps to change things. If the cause is more to do with personalities, or perhaps jealousy on your boss's part, you won't get a clear response. But highlighting the problem may well persuade them to lay off you.

- You can also use the techniques for dealing with a boss who humiliates you in public, and you may find that some of the other categories covered in this chapter apply to your boss.

...is a control freak

Control freaks are convinced that the job is only safe if it's in their hands. No one else can do it as well as them. Consequently they check up on you constantly, they tell you exactly how to do each task (only their way will do), and they delegate little or nothing. You feel stifled and unable to develop or expand your responsibilities.

- There's good news. The control freak is worried you can't do the job to their exacting standards. But in fact, almost every control freak has one or two chosen people who they *do* trust. These people are allowed to get on with the job, leaving the boss safe in the knowledge that it will be done just as they would have done it themselves. You just have to become one of the trusted few.

- The way to do this is to play their game better than they do. Give them a progress report even before they ask for it. Perform tasks exactly as the boss stipulates – you can even ask for their advice or guidance. Do your work logically, and copy your boss's style in such things as organising your time or keeping lists.

- Once your boss realises you are a team member after their own heart, they will gradually start trusting you to have more autonomy, or to take on new responsibilities. Don't expect to reach this point in a couple of weeks, but have patience, and be thorough in your work, and you'll get there in the end.

Give them a progress report even before they ask for it. Perform tasks exactly as the boss stipulates.

> **Ask for interference**
>
> Don't get defensive with control freaks, especially if there seems to be a level of personal mistrust (such as a conviction that you're fiddling your time sheet). Perversely, what you should do is encourage your boss to check up on you (no, that wasn't a misprint – I really did say 'encourage'). The point of this is that it will build your boss's trust in you and, although they may take the opportunity initially, they are more likely to loosen their hold once they see that you are trustworthy.

...is always right

This boss won't listen to anyone else's point of view. Why should they? They already know the right answer. And once they've made up their minds about something (which doesn't generally take long) the subject is closed. Period.

Working for this kind of boss is extremely constricting because they know exactly how to do your job, and they won't be happy if you don't do it the way they know is right. Here are the best ploys for dealing with the boss who's always right.

- Never tell them they're wrong. You've probably picked this one up already, but what do you do when they *are* wrong? The best way to get them to see it is by asking innocent questions: 'Can you explain how that will work in peak production periods?' 'I think I follow, but what happens after the initial promotion?' 'Could you just explain how that works with new staff?' Now sit back, and let your boss realise their error of judgement for themselves.

- If you have trouble wresting responsibility away from this expert, who knows how to do the job so much better than you, be realistic. Find the area of the job they find least interesting or consider least important, and ask to be allowed to make decisions over that. For example: 'I know Scotland is our smallest territory, and none of our big customers is there. Could I look after those regional accounts, with authority to agree discounts? There won't be any really big figures involved anyway, and I've been watching the way you handle customer discounts in the south east.' This way you can slowly build up a recognition in them that you know much of what they do, and must therefore be right quite often yourself.

- Bosses who are always right, and therefore never listen to anyone else, are actually wrong quite often (surprise, surprise). When this happens, resist the temptation to say, 'I told you so', and instead help your boss to save face: 'Of course, if it hadn't been a leap year, your projections for February would have been spot on.' There's a good reason for this. These people, once proved wrong, will always look for someone else to blame. (Obviously. It couldn't have been them, after all, because they're always right.) So align yourself with them fast, so the finger of blame points past you and elsewhere.

- Make sure you get things right as often as is humanly possible. Do your homework thoroughly, so that your results always demonstrate that you, too, are invariably right. Well, almost...you'll doubtless find that no one else is allowed to be quite perfect.

...stalls

These people are often friendly, affable and easy to get along with. But when you need a decision made, or need someone to put your case to senior management – or even just need advice – they somehow wriggle, stall, or just plain disappear.

Since they hate conflict, this boss is also very reluctant to give you constructive criticism or to put you straight if you go wrong.

Why stall?

Often the problem for these bosses is that they simply can't handle conflict. So rather than tell you that your proposal isn't considered good enough to implement, they just avoid making a decision on it. Or, worse, they send you off to do some extra research on it, or add another section, just to put off having to disappoint you. And it's not only you they don't want to get into deep water with. They are nervous of arguing with their own bosses. So when you ask them to clear a budget increase for you, they somehow never sort it out. They take no for an answer without putting up any reasoned defence, and leave you in an impossible position.

Since they hate conflict, this boss is also very reluctant to give you constructive criticism or to put you straight if you go wrong. Consequently, you may well have little idea if your performance isn't up to scratch. This is demoralising for you, and can be downright dangerous to your career if more senior managers can see the problem but your own boss hasn't enlightened you.

So what can you do to get these reluctant bosses to start doing their job properly? Here are a few techniques that will help.

- If you ask them for a straight opinion on your performance, they won't be able to make any negative comments. It might upset you. They'll just insist there's nothing wrong. So if you sense there's a problem, try phrasing your question differently: 'What do you think could improve my proposal to make it even better?' This allows them to feel they are being helpful rather than brutally honest, and they answer while still implying that the proposal was excellent.

- If your boss is stalling, there is some kind of conflict. Maybe they know that senior management don't want to see any budget increases this year. Or perhaps they feel that their own boss doesn't support the project you want the additional funds for. So get them to tell you what the conflict is – then you know what you're dealing with. And they may find it easier to tackle the situation once it's out in the open. Try saying, 'I realise there's a conflict for you here. I'm pushing for an increase for this budget. So what's on the other side, holding you back?'

- If your boss is simply indecisive and puts off making decisions, try acting as an unofficial adviser, and see if you can't help them to find a firm solution. Or simply make the decision yourself. Talk to them about the problem, and then say, 'That's really helpful. OK, I'll tell you what I'll do...' Make this a statement rather than a question. This gives them the chance to disagree, but almost certainly they will leave you to get on with it, having effectively approved your decision.

- Don't pressure this kind of boss too hard. If the pressure feels worse to them than the risk of doing something, they will do anything just to get you off their back. And it probably won't be what you want them to do.

...takes credit for *your* ideas

This is not only infuriating, it's also damaging to your career. If your good ideas aren't recognised as your own, how can you be rewarded for them? If you have one of these bosses, you need to take action to make sure you get the credit you deserve.

- For a start, keep records of your ideas and suggestions, and notes of relevant meetings with your boss. Send them memos and emails in order to elicit a written response. For example, send them an email saying, 'As I promised during our meeting about my idea for developing a motorised pushchair, here are the figures...' Any reply that doesn't argue with your mention of its being your idea clearly acknowledges the fact that it is.

- Get your ideas down as a formal proposal, with your name on the cover page, and the date.

- Let other people know about your ideas, either verbally or by copying to them anything you can justify, including your proposal.

> **Comments welcome**
>
> As well as getting your ideas and successes down in writing, try to elicit – and keep on file – any outside evidence to back you up. Testimonials from customers, emails from other managers offering thanks or praise, statistics showing how things have improved since you introduced your idea...all these go to show that the credit should be yours.

- After the idea has been proved a success, blow your own trumpet as much as you can. Let people know how pleased you are that your idea turned out to be a winner. While senior management may be the group you most want to notice you and recognise the idea as your own, it's worth telling anyone just to get your success widely circulated. So tell colleagues in other departments as well as your own, managers of other departments and so on.

- In order to avoid riling your boss, give them credit (even if you're not sure they really deserve it) for encouraging your idea. You may even feel you can send an email or memo to your boss's boss, saying how grateful you were for your boss's support for your idea.

...is dishonest

We've already looked at certain specific acts of dishonesty, such as passing the buck or stealing your credit. But what about telling lies to get out of trouble, or fiddling report sheets to make the figures look better? And what if your boss expects you to join in with this dishonesty?

- If you are not personally expected to get involved in the dishonesty, you'll have to use your own judgement to decide when things are serious enough for you to take action.

- Once you decide to do something, go to your boss. Don't take a moral tack or lecture them – simply tell them you are uncomfortable with the situation and feel you have to do something about it. This gives your boss a chance to stop doing whatever it is and you will let the matter rest.

- If your boss refuses to stop and you decide to take action, make sure you can prove your allegations of dishonesty. Your boss will very possibly deny it, and may well try to make you a scapegoat in some way. So secure your own position before going to whichever senior manager or department is appropriate.

- Should your boss try to involve you in the dishonesty, refuse without moralising. Tell them you're not prepared to be put in a position that could jeopardise your career. Remember, if the deceit is uncovered, your boss may well try to cast the blame in every direction but their own. And you'll be right in the firing line. From a career point of view, refusing to play ball will be far less damaging than getting involved.

Obviously there are certain kinds of dishonesty which you may feel call for you to blow the whistle at once, without giving your boss a chance to remedy things. Only you know when this type of serious action is called for.

If your boss refuses to stop and you decide to take action, make sure you can prove your allegations of dishonesty.

...believes in workaholism

If your boss wants to work 18 hours a day, it's really not your problem. But if you're expected to join in, it can be a big problem. And the more your colleagues play ball, the more isolated you will feel if you complain.

When in Rome

There are some industries where long hours are considered the norm. You may not like it, but it's no good becoming a theatre actor and then saying you don't want to work evenings, or a footballer and declining to play at the weekends. The trouble comes when colleagues in other departments get to work nine to five, but your boss expects longer hours.

- If it's not too late already, don't start working long hours. It's a lot easier to say no in the first place than to get fed up after a few months and try cutting your workload down by several hours a week.

- Talk to your boss, using feedback techniques (Chapter 9). If you can get the support of your team mates, this will be even more effective. But don't make it look like a mutiny – just a collective request for a rethink on the hours your department works. Explain that when you took this job on, you were led to believe the working hours were nine to five (or whatever they're supposed to be – check your contract to make sure of your facts). Don't come across as a jobsworth – you can say that you understand that it's not realistic to expect to leave work on the dot of five every day, but that working late seems to have become the norm, and it's making you feel demoralised and demotivated.

- Don't allow your boss to intimidate you into working unreasonably long hours. You are not paid to work these hours, so you have the right to refuse. Your boss has to recognise that you work extra hours out of goodwill. You can be assertive (see Chapter 7), explaining that you are not happy giving the organisation this many extra hours for nothing, and that you intend to reduce the work you do outside office hours.

- If you can come up with a reason for cutting down your hours, this will be a big help. It may genuinely be the thing that has spurred you to take action in the first place. Maybe you've just started a family, or an elderly parent suddenly needs more care, or you've been diagnosed with a stress-related illness.

- The biggest problem for your boss, in practical terms, will be that if you reduce your hours you will necessarily reduce the amount of work you get through each week. So do whatever you can to help. Improve your time management skills, delegate what you can, find ways to streamline tasks. You might discuss this option with your boss, and let them know you're aiming to reduce your hours without your work suffering.

- You can often cut your hours this way without reference to the boss. If they notice you're now knocking off at six instead of eight each evening, and try to give you an extra few hours' work a week to fill in the time, make it clear you've improved your effectiveness for your own benefit, not theirs.

- Expect it to take time to cut down your hours. Tell your boss, for example, that when this project is completed at the end of next month, you intend to avoid working such long hours again. You're not trying to get out of your existing workload, you're just planning to reduce it by natural wastage. You may need to do this in several stages, depending on the options and how many hours you're trying to cut.

- You'll need to recognise that your boss isn't likely to be happy with your working nine to five if no one else does. It might seem like plenty to you, but they'll see you as lazy. If you are otherwise happy with the job, and want to stay, find a reasonable compromise. Perhaps you could work half an hour later each day, with the occasional late evening for a special reason. Be prepared, however, for your boss's constant pressure to increase this, and be ready to decline tasks that won't fit into the working hours you're happy with.

Permanently on call?

If your boss is inclined to call you up out of hours, or even on holiday, make it impossible for them. Don't give them your number, or give them only your mobile number and turn it off whenever you can. Leave your answering machine on at home, or get someone else to answer calls. Make it clear you consider it an invasion of privacy being called out of hours. Tell them the place you're holidaying doesn't have a phone – or be straight and tell them it does but you're not giving them the number. And brief family and colleagues not to put the boss in touch with you.

...uses emotional blackmail

Emotional blackmail is unpleasant coming from anyone, and coming from your boss it can be particularly insidious. 'The whole team's going to be in a mess if you don't do this...' or 'Please don't let me down...' Your boss is playing on your desire to do well, contribute to the team and be successful, and trying to make you feel guilty if you don't co-operate.

- People who use emotional blackmail do it because it works. If you can show them it won't work with you, they'll learn to stop doing it in time. The way to counter emotional blackmail is by being assertive, without becoming aggressive.

- Recognise emotional blackmail when it's directed at you, and don't feel guilty. In fact, as soon as you sense feelings of guilt, ask yourself,

Anyone who stoops to emotional blackmail doesn't deserve a positive response.

'Am I being emotionally blackmailed?' If the answer is yes, dump the guilt.

- How do you dump it? It can be hard, but you need to remind yourself that emotional blackmail is a manipulative behaviour, and the person practising it should be the one to feel guilty, not you. Anyone who stoops to emotional blackmail doesn't deserve a positive response. Remind yourself, too, that if you can show them it doesn't work with you, you'll be setting a valuable example for other susceptible members of the team.

- Now just adopt the stuck record approach, 'I'm sorry, I can't do it' repeated until they get the message. If they ask why, try to avoid giving a detailed answer or you'll find yourself in a debate about it. At most just say, 'I'm sorry, I haven't time, I can't do it.'

Can the boss take a joke?

If you respond aggressively to emotional blackmail it will simply cause unpleasantness. But with some bosses you can get away with saying, jokingly, 'Careful, that's starting to sound like emotional blackmail...' They'll deny it, of course, but it will often make them back off when they realise they've been rumbled.

...or is simply never there

An absent boss probably sounds like heaven to some people – especially those whose boss is a control freak or a perfectionist. But in fact it carries its own problems. The reason you have a manager is presumably because you need one – to make decisions, authorise money and resources, and smooth the way when you need co-operation from other departments. All these things are hard to achieve when your boss is never around.

Most bosses' jobs take them out of the office from time to time. The problem arises when your boss seems to arrange endless appointments and trips away, and to be in a continuous stream of meetings when they *are* back at base. They should make sure there is time for their team to consult and talk to them when they need to, but not all of them do.

- Try feedback with your boss. They may be unaware of the problems they are causing, and if you explain the difficulties you have because they're rarely there, they may readily agree to be around for, say, a couple of hours twice a week, and available on the phone at least once every day.

- Whether or not they really change their ways as a result of the feedback session, you'll need to be as organised as possible to make the best of the time you have access to them. Anticipate what you're likely to need from them, so that when you do get to speak to them, you can sort out all the things you're going to need before the next time you see them. If they're not in the office again until Monday, be ready with all your requests for authorisation, decisions and so on for the rest of the week.

- Put all your requests as briefly as you can, so as not to waste what precious time you have with them. Try to put things in writing, such as proposals for ideas, figures to justify requests for money or other resources, and pros and cons with recommendations for any decisions you need them to approve.

- If you can put your requests in writing, you can also do yourself a favour by giving them to your boss as early as possible, and letting them know when you need a response. This way they can read them while they're away from the office.

- Use email as much as possible – it's the best way to communicate with someone you hardly see face-to-face, and it gives them very little excuse not to get back to you.

- And what if your boss is so busy they never get back to you, and being absent you can't collar them and wring an answer out of them? If you email proposals, figures for authorisation, points for decision or anything else that requires a response, explain in the covering email that you need a response or decision by a certain date. Then say something like, 'As you'll see from the attached figures, we really can't tackle this project successfully without increasing the budget to £8,000. I need to commission the design work next week, so if I haven't heard back from you by the end of Friday, I'll assume I should go ahead on the basis of a budget of £8,000.' In other words, always indicate that you'll take a lack of response as a yes, or a no, or whatever you stipulate. With an email to back you up, they really can't argue if they do nothing and you carry right on.

More power to your
[business-mind]

Even at the end there's more we can learn. More that *we* can learn from your experience of this book, and more ways to add to *your* learning experience.

For who to read, what to know and where to go in the world of business, visit us at **business-minds.com**.

Here you can find out more about the people and ideas that can make you and your business more innovative and productive. Each month our e-newsletter, *Business-minds Express*, delivers an infusion of thought leadership, guru interviews, new business practice and reviews of key business resources directly to you. Subscribe for free at

● **www.business-minds.com/goto/newsletters**

Here you can also connect with ways of putting these ideas to work. Spreading knowledge is a great way to improve performance and enhance business relationships. If you found this book useful, then so might your colleagues or customers. If you would like to explore corporate purchases or custom editions personalised with your brand or message, then just get in touch at

● **www.business-minds.com/corporatesales**

We're also keen to learn from your experience of our business books – so tell us what you think of this book and what's on *your* business mind with an online reader report at business-minds.com. Together with our authors, we'd like to hear more from you and explore new ways to help make these ideas work at

● **www.business-minds.com/goto/feedback**

[www.business-minds.com
www.financialminds.com]